BEST OF

Las Vegas

Andrew Dean Nystrom

Best of Las Vegas
2nd edition – March 2005
First published – May 2003

Published by Lonely Planet Publications Pty Ltd
ABN 36 005 607 983

Australia	Head Office, Locked Bag 1, Footscray, Vic 3011
	☎ 03 8379 8000 fax 03 8379 8111
	🖳 talk2us@lonelyplanet.com.au
USA	150 Linden St, Oakland, CA 94607
	☎ 510 893 8555 toll free 800 275 8555
	fax 510 893 8572
	🖳 info@lonelyplanet.com
UK	72–82 Rosebery Avenue, London EC1R 4RW
	☎ 020 7841 9000 fax 020 7841 9001
	🖳 go@lonelyplanet.co.uk

This title was commissioned in Lonely Planet's Oakland
office and produced by: **Commissioning Editor** Suki
Gear **Coordinating Editor** Kate McLeod **Coordinating
Cartographers** Amanda Sierp, Herman So, Jolyon Philcox
& Kusnandar **Layout Designer** Brendan Dempsey **Editor**
Victoria Harrison **Managing Cartographer** Alison Lyall
Cover Designers Pepi Bluck, Yukiyoshi Kamimura **Project
Manager** Charles Rawlings-Way **Mapping Development**
Paul Piaia **Thanks to** Anthony Phelan, Eoin Dunlevy,
Glenn Beanland, Melanie Dankel, Sonya Brooke

Photographs by Lonely Planet Images and Ray Laskowitz
except for the following: p16, Neil Setchfield; p34, Ralph
Lee Hopkins; p81 Lee Foster/Lonely Planet Images. **Cover
photograph** Welcome to fabulous Las Vegas, Nevada, Neil
Setchfield/Lonely Planet Images. All images are copyright
of the photographers unless otherwise indicated. Many of
the images in this guide are available for licensing from
Lonely Planet Images: 🖳 www.lonelyplanetimages.com

ISBN 1 74059 853 9

Printed by Markono Print Media Pte Ltd, Singapore

HOW TO USE THIS BOOK

Color-Coding & Maps

Each chapter has a color code along the
banner at the top of the page which is also
used for text and symbols on maps (eg all
venues reviewed in the Highlights chapter
are orange on the maps). The fold-out
maps inside the front and back covers are
numbered from 1 to 4. All sights and venues
in the text have map references; eg (2, C4)
means Map 2, grid reference C4. See p96 for
map symbols.

Prices

Multiple prices listed with reviews (eg $10/5)
usually indicate adult/concession admission to
a venue. Concession prices can include senior,
student, member or coupon discounts. Meal
cost and room rate categories are listed at
the start of the Eating and Sleeping chapters,
respectively.

Text Symbols

☎	telephone
✉	address
🖳	email/website address
$	admission
☉	opening hours
ⓘ	information
Ⓜ	monorail
🚌	bus
🚊	tram
Ⓟ	parking available
♿	wheelchair access
✕	on site/nearby eatery
⚹	child-friendly venue
Ⓥ	good vegetarian selection

Contents

From the Publisher

AUTHOR

Andrew Dean Nystrom

Born a mile high in Denver, Colorado, Andrew has traversed the Mojave Desert many times while criss-crossing the Western USA in search of outdoor adventure. An inveterate night owl, he could not resist the opportunity to investigate what makes the world's most insomniac playground tick. He has contributed text and images to many Lonely Planet titles. Andrew wrote the first edition of *Las Vegas Condensed* and his newspaper bylines include the *Miami Herald* and *San Francisco Chronicle*. His writing has been translated into a dozen languages. Andrew was last spotted shipping out for the wide-open wildlands of Argentine and Chilean Patagonia. Find more of his work at www .guidebookwriters.com or contact him via laughtears@gmail.com.

Many thanks to Morgan, my parents, Joe and Dolores, Suki Gear, Erin Corrigan, Katrina Browning, Karen Silveroli, Angela Torres and Jen Leo.

PHOTOGRAPHER

Ray Laskowitz

Ray has been making pictures for almost 30 years both in the United States and through most of Asia and a bit of Europe. His imagery is a unique blend of photojournalistic decisive moments and artistic feeling and movement. For Ray, working in Las Vegas was enjoyable since many of his images depend on light and intense color for their impact. And, certainly, Las Vegas even during the daylight hours is a colorful city.

SEND US YOUR FEEDBACK

We love to hear from travellers – your comments keep us on our toes and help make our books better. Our well-travelled team reads every word on what you loved or loathed about this book. Although we cannot reply individually to postal submissions, we always guarantee that your feedback goes straight to the appropriate authors, in time for the next edition – and the most useful submissions are rewarded with a free book. To send us your updates – and find out about Lonely Planet events, newsletters and travel news – visit our award-winning website: 🖳 **www.lonelyplanet.com/feedback.**

Note: We may edit, reproduce and incorporate your comments in Lonely Planet products such as guidebooks, websites and digital products, so let us know if you don't want your comments reproduced or your name acknowledged. For a copy of our privacy policy visit 🖳 www.lonelyplanet.com/privacy.

Introducing Las Vegas

Las Vegas is a city condensed – in time, space and history. Three sleep-less days here begin to feel like a week. It's glitz and glam for its own sake, over-the-top cash and flash as both a means and an end. As such,

the city demands a suspension of disbelief – the moment you begin to take it seriously you totally miss the point.

It's also a huge uninhibited adult playground. Big money. Gambling. Strip clubs. Hip, sexy nightlife. Luxurious spa pamper-ing. Gourmet Rabelaisian feasts. Glamorous designer shopping. Out-of-this-world adrenaline rushes. Cheap thrills. Whatever you desire, North America's fastest-growing metropolis and its monolithic megaresorts stand ready to cater to your every whim 24/7. Ultimately, Sin City exists, as in the deserts of the Bible, as a place for pilgrims to cast off their iniquities.

Today's adolescent Las Vegas – coming of age and trying to clean up its act, but not quite mature yet – is like a spoiled kid who is always playing dress-up. It's a self-assured brat with no idea what it wants to be when it grows up, but certain it's going to be fabulously rich and famous some day. Like every world-class destination, at the end of the day, Vegas is whatever you want it to be.

It's only a matter of time before some brash, self-referential impresario erects a scale-model replica of Las Vegas itself. Try as they may, no-one will ever be able to replicate the original.

Traffic trawls The Strip

Neighborhoods

Paradoxically, Las Vegas is physically isolated from neighboring metropolises like Los Angeles, yet, in our jet-set age, it's the world's second-most popular tourist destination, after Paris. Two interstate highways (I-15 and US Hwy 95) bisect the town. If it's your first time in town and you're driving, make sure you do a few things. First, arrive at night. Next, pull over and admire everything from afar before you hit the city limits. Finally, take the first exit and cruise the length of The Strip.

In a very real sense, there are two Las Vegases: **Downtown** sits at the north end of the tourist corridor, with **Glitter Gulch** (and the Fremont Street Experience) streaking down its middle. The city's original quarter attracts far fewer onlookers and is preferred by serious gamblers who find white tigers and faux volcanoes beneath them. The smoky, low-ceilinged casinos have changed little over the years, and as attractions, they've got little to offer nongamblers.

The desolate area along **Las Vegas Blvd** (aka The Strip), known as Naked City, links Downtown with the **Upper Strip**, which begins at the Stratosphere. Treasure Island and the Venetian mark the start of the **Lower Strip**, which runs south past Mandalay Bay to the airport.

As the cliché goes, **The Strip** is constantly reinventing itself. Every megaresort is an attraction, with plenty on offer besides gambling. This newer, brighter, shinier center of gravity is an adult Disneyland, dealing nonstop excitement. With each new development it becomes more spectacular (and more of a spectacle).

Few short-term visitors venture beyond The Strip, where some of the best bars, live music and ethnic food await. The less glitzy **Eastside** and **Westside** are the domain of locals, while the area around the **University of Nevada** (UNLV) campus attracts more carpetbaggers.

Disorientation is a constant risk, whether it be while searching for your room, wending your way through a purposefully confusing hotel-casino or trying to remember where you parked the car.

> ### Off the Beaten Track
> Where to go to get away from the incessant ding-ding-ding? Public parks are few and far between. If you don't fancy a round of golf (p87) or bowling (p74), stroll through an upscale shopping arcade (pp37-9), climb above it all at the Eiffel Tower (p21) or the Stratosphere (p22), take a road trip (pp33-4) or visit University of Nevada's Marjorie Barrick Museum (p27).

High and mighty – Hoover Dam

Itineraries

If you haven't visited Vegas recently, you can't claim to know Americas' fastest-growing metropolis. Most new must-sees front The Strip, but when you grow weary of all the glitz, it's worth checking out the vintage vibe Downtown.

Many visitors never make it beyond the comfy confines of their hotel. That's fine if you're staying at an all-inclusive megaresort like the Bellagio or MGM. Even then, it's best to escape the casinos and stretch your legs (and lungs) a bit, even if only for a walking tour (p30-3) or monorail ride (p83).

Worst of Las Vegas
- Traffic gridlock on The Strip
- Long buffet, check-in and nightclub lines
- Cigar smoke and poor ventilation in casinos
- Colossal convention crowds that send rates soaring

One Day

Cruise The Strip then hit the megaresorts for a taste of the casino action. Ride the monorail between properties, with stopovers for noshing and shopping. After a gourmet dinner, catch a late Cirque du Soleil show (pp65-6) then party until dawn.

Two Days

Wake up on The Strip with a spot of brunch (p47). Relax by the pool (p24) or luxuriate at a spa (p25) – it's going to be another late night. Rent a convertible (pp84-5) and roll east to Hoover Dam (p33). After a cat nap, dine with a celebrity chef then sup a nightcap at an ultralounge with a view (pp61-2).

Three Days

Sleep in, then detour Downtown to see where it all began. Sidle up to a buffet at a classy carpet joint. Stroll Fremont St after sunset to experience the Experience (p20), then check out the illuminating Neon Museum (p28). After sunset, revisit The Strip to let it ride one last time.

Highlights

BELLAGIO (2, C4)

Inspired by the beauty of the lakeside Italian village, and built by Steve Wynn on the site of the legendary Dunes, the $1.6 billion Bellagio is Vegas' original opulent, if parvenu, pleasure palazzo. Its Tuscan architecture and 8-acre **artificial lake** – the antithesis of what most people expect of Las Vegas – is, in a word, elegant. The view you get from The Strip is of a green-blue lake from which spring a thousand dancing **fountains**.

INFORMATION
- ☎ 693-7111
- 🖥 www.bellagio.com
- ✉ 3600 Las Vegas Blvd S
- ⓘ fountain shows every 15min 7pm-midnight daily & every 30min 3-7pm Mon-Fri, noon-7pm Sat & Sun
- 🚝 to/from Monte Carlo (under construction)
- Ⓜ Paris & Bally's
- ✖ see pp47-8

Twinkling, dancing fountains

DON'T MISS
- The free choreographed Lake Como fountain show
- Dale Chihuly's *Fiori di Como* sculpture on the lobby ceiling
- Original artwork in Picasso (p48) restaurant
- Aquatic exuberance – Cirque du Soleil's *O* (p66)

At the water's edge is a cluster of buildings that have seemingly been plucked from the Lake District. Beyond the glass and metal **porte cochere**, inside the 36-floor resort, are a stable of world-class **gourmet restaurants** (pp47-8), a swish **shopping concourse** (p39), the **Gallery of Fine Art** (p27) and a **European-style casino**.

The highlight of the hotel's **stunning lobby** is the 18ft ceiling, which is adorned with a backlit **glass sculpture** composed of 2000 hand-blown flowers in vibrant colors. Real flowers, cultivated in a gigantic on-site greenhouse, brighten countless vases throughout the property. Adjacent to the lobby, the **Conservatory and Botanical Gardens** host dazzling seasonal floral arrangements, which are installed by crane through the soaring 50ft ceiling.

In the courtyard, the distinctive swimming-pool area is surrounded by private cabanas and accented by artfully formed citrus and parterre-style gardens. The Mediterranean villa setting makes for a pleasant stroll, but use of the facilities by nonguests is limited. In 2005, a new luxury Spa Tower and expanded spa facilities will be the lavish icing atop the five-diamond cake. Baby strollers and unaccompanied children under 18 are not allowed at the Bellagio.

24/7/365 Megaresorts
Unless noted, all Highlights are always open, don't charge admission, offer free self-service and valet (tip $2) parking, are on CAT's 301/302 bus lines and are wheelchair accessible.

VENETIAN (2, C3)

Impresario Sheldon Adelson broke ground on his replica of La Serenissima (Most Serene Republic) – reputed to be the home of the world's first casino – shortly after the controversial and dramatic implosion of the 44-year-old Sands in 1996.

His $1.5 billion, 35-story copy of a doge's palace, inspired by the splendor of Italy's most-romantic city, is being developed in two phases. Phase I opened in 1999 with 3036 roomy suites, a 120,000-sq-ft casino and the sprawling **Grand Canal Shoppes** (p38) retail complex. The newest addition is the all-suite **Venezia Tower**, with its exclusive concierge level. Phase II of the Palazzo project will add 3000 more luxury suites to the property, making it the world's largest resort – if the Genting Highlands' planned 10,000 rooms in Kuala Lumpur aren't finished first.

INFORMATION
- ☎ 414-1000, 877-883-6423
- 🖳 www.venetian.com
- ✉ 3355 Las Vegas Blvd S
- ⓘ same-day, in-person gondola reservations required (☎ 414-4500), adult $12.50-15, child $5-7.50, private 2-passenger rides $50-60
- Ⓜ Harrah's & Imperial Palace
- ✕ see pp53-4

A **gondola-filled lagoon** and full-scale reproductions of Venetian landmarks like **Saint Marks Square** abound. Graceful bridges, flowing canals, vibrant piazzas and welcoming stone walkways capture the Venetian spirit in faithful detail. The casino is linked to the ever-expanding, state-of-the-art **Sands Expo & Convention Center**.

DON'T MISS
- Romantic private Grand Canal gondola rides
- Roaming mimes and minstrels in period costume
- Hand-painted ceiling frescoes near the casino entrance
- A moisturizing body-cocoon treatment at Canyon Ranch SpaClub

Other amenities include the world-class **Canyon Ranch Spa-Club** (p25) and fitness center, top-drawer gourmet restaurants and the stunning **Guggenheim Hermitage Museum** (p27).

Even if you've had the good fortune to stroll the cobblestones and ply the romantic canals of the one-and-only Italian port, you won't want to miss the Vegas version. In a city filled with spectacles, the Venetian is surely one of the most spectacular.

Newer, Bigger, Better...
'Pardon Our Dust' signs greet visitors all over town. Ongoing blockbuster construction projects include the $2.7 billion Wynn Las Vegas resort (p72), the $1.6 billion Palazzo tower next to the Venetian and the $375 million Caesars Palace expansion. Sans irony, bankrupt developer Donald Trump has proposed a megabucks 64-story hotel-condo tower near the Frontier Hotel.

CAESARS PALACE (2, C4)

Vegas' first fully-realized megaresort upped the luxury ante for the gaming industry when it debuted in 1966. Thanks to ongoing megabucks renovations, Caesars is redefining its swanky self and is as impressive as ever. Despite the upgrades, the Palace remains, for many, quintessentially Vegas.

INFORMATION
- ☎ 731-7110, 877-427-7243
- 🖥 www.caesarspalace.com
- ✉ 3570 Las Vegas Blvd S
- ℹ hourly fountain shows in Forum Shops
- Ⓜ Flamingo & Caesars Palace
- ✕ see pp48-9

The Greco-Roman fantasyland captured the world's attention with its full-size **marble reproductions of classical statuary**, its Stripside row of **towering fountains** and its cocktail waitresses costumed as goddesses. Bar girls continue to roam the gaming areas in skimpy togas, and the fountains are still out front – the same ones daredevil Evil Knievel made famous when he jumped them on a motorcycle on December 31, 1967. In 2000, the lawns and gardens were enlarged, and Corinthian columns and the stately **Garden of the Gods** pool complex were added. Inside, neon and cheesy mirrors were replaced with hand-painted murals.

Two central **casinos** contain a hundred card tables and a couple of thousand slots that will accept up to $500 chips. The state-of-the-art **race and sports book** has 90 video screens. Other attractions include a movie theater with a dome-shaped screen, three live-entertainment lounges and the upscale **Forum Shops** (p38) concourse, featuring an impressive aquarium and animatronic fountain shows. **The Colosseum**, a new 4000-seat showroom modeled after its Roman namesake, debuted in 2003 with a **Céline Dion** theatrical spectacle, conceived by ex–Cirque du Soleil director Franco Dragone (p65).

With the expansion of the pool complex, the new outdoor Roman Plaza and completion of a new luxury tower, Caesars appears poised to rule the empire once again.

DON'T MISS
- Sexy silhouettes at the Shadow Bar
- Four-ton Brahma shrine near the front entrance
- Animatronic fountain shows in Forum Shops (p38)
- Free beneath-the-scenes tours at Forum Shops aquarium
- Neoclassical statue reproductions, including Michelangelo's *David*

Stylish shopping at Caesars

MANDALAY BAY   (2, C6)

Vegas' megaresorts have long sought to boost their appeal by inviting celebrity chefs to set up shop under their roofs. The $950 million, tropically themed 'M-Bay' is no exception. However when legendary tenor Luciano Pavarotti played a grand opening concert at the **Events Center** (p69) in 1999, it carried this bundling strategy three steps further by adding a **House of Blues** (p63) entertainment complex and the exclusive **Foundation Room** (p62), and by renting out its 35th through 39th floors to the **Four Seasons** (p71) resort chain.

INFORMATION
- ☎ 632-7777, 877-632-7800
- 🖥 www.mandalaybay.com
- ✉ 3950 Las Vegas Blvd S
- 🚝 to/from Luxor & Excalibur
- ✖ see pp50-1

Standouts among M-Bay's attractions include **Shark Reef** aquarium complex, home to thousands of submarine beasties and a shallow pool where you can pet pint-sized sharks. Other rare and endangered toothy reptiles are on display in the fun, if overpriced, compound. Rather save your money for the slots? Check out the two free and very impressive **aquariums**, one near the registration desk and the other at the Coral Reef Lounge. Gamblers will appreciate the vast and classy **casino** and **race and sports book**. The main nightspot **rumjungle** (p50) features walls of fire at its entrance and a huge tower of firewaters for sampling.

DON'T MISS
- Championship boxing at the Events Center
- Folk art at the Foundation Room and House of Blues
- Wine stewards scaling a four-story tower at Aureole (p50)
- Lenin statue, vodka locker, solid ice bar & sable coats at Red Square (p50)

Outside, an **11-acre garden** complex includes a **sand-and-surf beach** (open spring and summer for surfing competitions on 6ft waves), a lazy river ride, a variety of pools, and the Euro-style Moorea Beach Club and ultralounge. **THEhotel** (p71) and the **Mandalay Place** (p72) shopping promenade are the latest stylish additions.

Lady Luck Goes Digital

Like everything else, slot machines have entered the digital age. Microchips are replacing spring-driven reels, and the random selection of symbols now takes a split second. How has the microchip changed the billion-dollar slot industry? For one thing, it allows slots to be networked, creating 'progressive' jackpots in the tens of millions of dollars. It allows for slot-club cards that reward regular players with prizes. It also allows casinos to constantly track their machines, and to make them as entertaining as video games. Some machines are now 'cable ready,' letting players watch their favorite soap operas.

TREASURE ISLAND (2, C3)

Yo, ho, whoa: though traces of Treasure Island's (TI) original swash-buckling skull-and-crossbones theme linger (if you look hard), the new-look terra-cotta–toned resort now strives for an 'elegant Caribbean hideaway' feel – with 'leave the kids at home' implied. TI's shift away from family-friendly, to bawdy and naughty, epitomizes Vegas' on-going efforts to put the 'sin' back in 'casino.' One-armed Playboy bandits now await where playful pirates, plastic doubloons and chests full-o-booty once reigned.

INFORMATION

- ☎ 894-7111, 800-944-7444
- 🖳 www.treasureisland .com
- ✉ 3300 Las Vegas Blvd S
- ⓘ *Sirens of TI* show every 90min 7-11:30pm Mon-Sat (weather permitting)
- 🚃 to/from Mirage
- ✗ Canter's Deli, Dishes Buffet, Isla

Hunt for buried treasure.

Visitors approach the property via a wood-bottomed bridge with hemp rope supporting sides (for that 'authentic' piratey feel!) that spans the artificial Sirens' Cove, beside which is a replica of an **18th-century sea village**. The spiced-up **Sirens of TI** mock sea battle, a clash of the sexes pitting sultry temptresses against renegade freebooters, takes place in the cove fronting the entryway. In the harbor, two ships – a privateer vessel and a British frigate – face off on schedule several times nightly.

The hideaway theme continues inside the sprawling **casino**, where the slot machines and gaming tables are tightly grouped but no-one seems to mind. Thankfully, the relentless theme is toned down in the four-diamond guestrooms. Recent grown-up additions include deluxe poolside cabanas, a huge party-friendly hot tub and the Stripfront **Tangerine** burlesque lounge and nightclub (p62).

The real must-see here is Cirque du Soleil's fantastic evening production, **Mystère** (p65). Easing the journey there or back is a tram ride to the **Mirage** (p14), which shares the 100-acre site. Watch for a new skybridge linking TI and the Fashion Show Mall (p38).

DON'T MISS

- Easiest valet and self-service parking on The Strip
- Waterfalls in the lushly land-scaped swimming-pool complex
- Burlesque dancers and exotic cocktails at Tangerine during the *Sirens of TI* show

MGM GRAND (2, C5)

With over 5000 rooms, the $1 billion MGM retains the 'world's largest hotel' title, despite mounting competition from the Genting Highlands resort complex in Kuala Lumpur. Despite its size, the shimmering emerald-green 'City of Entertainment' does a decent job of making its attractions seem intimate.

MGM (owned by movie mogul Metro Goldwyn Mayer) has accomplished this feat by co-opting themes from Hollywood movies. The most obvious example is the resort's nightclub, **Studio 54** (p62). The adjacent **casino** consists of one gigantic, circular room with an **ornate domed ceiling** and replicated 1930s glamor replete with a bandstand featuring live jazz and

INFORMATION
- ☎ 891-1111, 877-880-0880
- 🖳 www.mgmgrand.com
- ✉ 3799 Las Vegas Blvd S
- ⓘ lion habitat open 11am-10pm
- Ⓜ MGM Grand
- ✘ see p51

swing nightly. At 171,500 sq ft, MGM Grand's gaming area is equal in size to four football fields and offers a whopping selection of slots and the full spectrum of table games, plus the requisite **race and sports book**, a poker room and a keno lounge.

Out front, it's hard to miss the **USA's largest bronze statue**, a 100,000lb lion that's 45ft tall, perched atop a 25ft pedestal and ringed by lush landscaping, fountains and Atlas-themed statues. Other attractions include the **lion habitat** (p29), two **shopping concourses** (pp38-9), the gigantic **Grand Garden Arena** (p69) that often hosts championship boxing bouts and megaconcerts, the saucy **La Femme** (p65) topless revue and an impressive celebrity chef line-up.

A new resident Cirque du Soleil show promises to up the theatrical ante in 2005. With so much to do here, many guests choose not to spend their time anywhere else.

Chump Change

When the MGM opened in December 1993, $3.5 million in quarters were needed for its slot machines and to provide change. Thirty-nine armored cars were hired to transport the 14 million coins, which were delivered in 3600 sacks. Each sack weighed 60lb.

MIRAGE (2, C3)

When the Mirage opened in 1989, then-owner Steve Wynn boasted that his goal was to create a property 'so overriding in its nature that it would be a reason in and of itself for visitors to come to Las Vegas.' This $630 million resort, also owned by MGM, is such a place. It's tropical setting, replete with a **huge atrium** filled with jungle foliage, meandering creeks and soothing cascades captures the imagination.

> **INFORMATION**
> ☎ 791-7111, 800-374-9000
> 🖥 www.mirage.com
> ✉ 3400 Las Vegas Blvd S
> ℹ volcano erupts every 15min 7pm–midnight, tiger habitat open 24hr
> 🚋 to/from Treasure Island
> Ⓜ Harrah's & Imperial Palace
> ✈ see p51

Woven into this waterscape are scores of bromeliads enveloped in sunlight and fed by a computerized misting system. Circling the atrium is a huge **Polynesian-themed casino**, which incorporates the unique design concept of placing gaming areas under separate roofs to invoke a feeling of intimacy. Real and faux tropical plants add to the splendor of the elegant casino, which also boasts a popular **high-stakes poker room**.

The registration area features an awesome **20,000-gallon saltwater aquarium** filled with 90 species of tropical critters, including pufferfish, manta rays and pygmy sharks. Acclaimed impressionist Danny Gans and touring comedians like Jay Leno provide the evening entertainment. Although the dynamic duo are no longer performing see the boxed text on p66), you can still visit **Siegfried & Roy's Secret Garden & Dolphin Habitat** (p29).

At the casino's south entrance, slanted glass at the **royal white tiger habitat** permits a glare-free view of a parade of big cats, which are rotated among several lovely habitats. Out front in the 3-acre lagoon, the fiery trademark **faux volcano** erupts frequently with a roar, inevitably bringing traffic on The Strip to a screeching halt.

> **DON'T MISS**
> • Tropical scents in the lobby lagoon
> • Feeding time at the tiger habitat
> • Live music in the lush Ava lounge
> • Fondling the bronze mermaids near the front door for good luck

PARIS (2, C4)

Napoleon once said, 'Secrets travel fast in Paris.' The same can be said for Las Vegas, where Paris, which opened in 1999, was one secret that made the rounds here in record time. This $785 million Gallic caricature evokes the gaiety of the City of Light – right down to wandering minstrels playing accordion music. The 34-story replica of the Hotel de Ville strives to capture the essence of the grand dame by re-creating her landmarks. Fine likenesses of the **Opéra House**, the **Arc de Triomphe**, **Champs-Élysées**, **Parc Monceau** and even the **River Seine** frame the property. Just like in the French capital, the signature attraction is the ersatz **Eiffel Tower** (p21).

INFORMATION
- ☎ 946-7000,
  877-796-2096
- 🖳 www.parislv.com
- ✉ 3655 Las Vegas Blvd S
- Ⓜ Bally's & Paris
- ✗ see pp52-3

Surrounded by street scenes from the Seine's Left and Right Banks, the bustling 85,000-sq-ft, high-ceilinged **casino** is home to a hundred gaming tables, a couple of thousand slot machines and a popular **sports bar** and **race and sports book**. A dozen French **restaurants du quartier** dish out authentic gourmet fare. **Le Cabaret** features live French- and English-style entertainment, while **Napoleons** champagne bar showcases jazz and popular-music bands. **Le Théatre des Arts** (p64) hosts the crème de la crème of international acts.

DON'T MISS
- Caviar facials at the Spa by Mandara
- How-to touchscreen gaming-video kiosks
- Wandering mimes, magicians and sword-swallowers
- Alfresco Strip-side drinks at Mon Ami Gabi (p53)
- The USA's only authentic French roulette wheel in a high-limit area (it has no '00')

Paris is adjacent to Bally's (p22). They are connected by an extension of the quaint cobblestone **Rue de la Paix** (p39) shopping promenade, which provides relatively easy access to the new monorail station.

NEW YORK-NEW YORK (2, C5)

Give me your tired, huddled (over a Wheel of Fortune slot machine) masses. Opened in 1997, this $485 million mini-megapolis features scaled-down replicas of the **Empire State Building** (47 stories or 529ft); the **Statue of Liberty**, ringed by a 9/11 memorial; a mini version of the **Brooklyn Bridge**; a Coney Island–style roller coaster called **Manhattan Express** (p21); and renditions of the **Chrysler**, **AT&T** and **CBS buildings**. Manhattan-a-phobes beware: it really can feel like Central Park on a sunny Sunday afternoon.

INFORMATION
- ☎ 740-6969, 888-693-6763
- 🖳 www.nynyhotel casino.com
- ✉ 3790 Las Vegas Blvd S
- Ⓜ MGM Grand
- ✕ see pp52-3

The attention to detail is remarkable, down to the whiffs of steam rising from faux manhole covers near the **Chrysler elevator**. This Disneyfied version of the Big Apple can get even more crowded than the real deal: around 200,000 pedestrians stride NYC's Brooklyn Bridge each year, but more than five million traverse the Vegas version.

The crowded **casino** attracts a mélange of (mostly middle American) humanity. Slews of slots and gaming tables are set against a rich backdrop of famous landmarks. Down with off-track betting? The **race and sports book** offers electronic satellite wagering. Restaurants and retail shops hide behind colorful facades from **Park Avenue**, **Greenwich Village** and **Times Square** storefronts.

What would a big bad city be without a few watering holes? The **Big Apple Bar** hosts live lounge acts; **Bar at Times Square** (p59) is popular with the 30-something crowd; while the **Nine Fine Irishmen** pub features well-poured pints and live jig bands. Cirque du Soleil's **Zumanity** (p65) titillates couples, and comedians such as Rita Rudner (p66), split sides with their shows.

DON'T MISS
- Ornate casino-level Rockefeller restrooms
- Playful USA bas-relief map in America eatery
- Coney Island Emporium arcade on 2nd level
- A stroll through Manhattan – without the mugging

STRATOSPHERE (2, D1)

Las Vegas has many buildings exceeding 20 stories, but only one tops a hundred. At 1149ft, the white, three-legged $550-million **Stratosphere Tower** is the tallest building in the USA, west of the Mississippi River. At its base is a **casino** that has all the trappings of a sprawling gaming room, but little in the way of a theme. There's a huge **swimming complex** and **adults-only beach club**.

However it's what's atop the elegantly tapered tower that people have been flocking to see since 1996. Here you'll find a **revolving restaurant** (p53), a **circular bar**, and indoor and outdoor **viewing decks** affording the best 360-degree panoramas in town.

INFORMATION
- ☎ 380-7777, 800-998-6937
- 🖥 www.stratospherehotel.com
- ✉ 2000 Las Vegas Blvd S
- ✖ Top of the World (p53)

DON'T MISS
- Views of The Strip from the pool complex
- Dancing light show atop the Tower
- Loose slots and video poker machines
- Retro-futuristic 1964 World's Fair–themed Strat-O-Fair midway arcade

To get you there, the Stratosphere boasts **America's fastest elevators**: they ascend and descend at 20.5mph, or about three times the speed of regular elevators, lifting you 108 floors in a mere 37 ear-popping seconds. Once you've recovered, head for the **High Roller** (p22), the world's highest roller coaster, but a bit of a letdown. Rising above it all is the **Big Shot** (p22), a highly recommended ride that really gets the blood rushing, by rocketing riders up and down the steel spire that forms the pinnacle of the tower. Try the rides at night for maximum effect.

Not to be forgotten are the Stratosphere's two good-value, if cheesy, production shows: celebrity impersonators in **American Superstars** and the long-running daytime cabaret **Viva Las Vegas**. The 3600-seat **outdoor events center** hosts rock concerts and championship boxing.

Size Matters
Consider some current world's records that Las Vegas holds:
- Largest atrium – Luxor (p18)
- Biggest hotel – MGM Grand (p13)
- Most-powerful beacon – Luxor (p18)
- Highest roller coaster – High Roller (p22)
- Biggest gold nugget – Hand of Faith (pp23–4)
- Largest sports book – Las Vegas Hilton (p24)
- Largest public wine collection – Rio's Wine Cellar (pp25–6)

LUXOR (2, C6)

Named after Egypt's splendid ancient city, which is perched on the east bank of the Nile, the landmark Luxor may have the greatest wow factor of all The Strip's megaresorts. The resort's designers chose a theme

INFORMATION
☎ 262-4000,
  888-777-0188
🖥 www.luxor.com
✉ 3900 Las Vegas Blvd S
🚝 to/from Excalibur &
  Mandalay Bay
🍴 Pharaoh's Pheast
  Buffet

that easily could have ended up a pyramid of gaudiness, but instead resulted in an elegant shrine to all things Egyptian. The pyramid houses the **world's largest atrium**, has 120,000 sq ft of smartly arranged gaming areas and hosts a diverse array of attractions.

Built in 1993, the focus is the **30-story pyramid** cloaked in black glass from base to apex; in all, there are 26,783 glass plates totaling 570,000 sq ft. The atrium is so voluminous it could accommodate nine Boeing 747s and still have room for 50 Cessnas. At its apex, a **40-billion-candlepower beacon**, the world's most powerful – sends a shaft of blue and white light 10 miles into space, where it's visible by astronauts

Out in front of the pyramid is a 10-story **crouching sphinx** and a sandstone obelisk etched with hieroglyphics. The pyramid's interior is tastefully decorated with many enormous Egyptian statues of guards, lions and rams; sand-

DON'T MISS
• The Blue Man Group (p65)
• 24/7 massages and facials
• IMAX theater and Ridefilm
• Pleasuredome at Ra nightclub (p62)
• Games of the Gods interactive arcade

stone walls adorned with hieroglyphic-inscribed tapestries and grand columns; a stunning replica of the great Temple of Ramses II and a pharaoh's treasure of polished marble.

There's a **casino**, of course, featuring a few thousand slot and video machines, over a hundred gaming tables, poker, keno and a cutting-edge **race and sports book**; the club **Ra** (p62) and a **King Tut museum** (p27).

King Tut at Luxor (and you thought it was in Egypt)

MAIN STREET STATION (3, D3)

The most charming of Downtown's establishments, and built in the 1970s, Main Street Station re-creates Victorian opulence with detailed craftsmanship, old-fashioned elegance and an extensive collection of antiques, architectural artifacts and collectibles. Throughout the lovely hotel and 28,000-sq-ft casino are notable *objets d'histoire*, most keeping to the turn-of-the-20th-century theme; then there are the other pieces of history, such as a large graffiti-covered **chunk of the Berlin Wall** above the urinals in the men's room.

Other artifacts on display include **Buffalo Bill Cody's private rail car**, which he used to travel the USA with his Wild West Show from 1906 until his death in 1917; three exquisite **bronze chandeliers** above the casino's central pit, which were originally installed in the 1890s at Coca-Cola's headquarters in Austin, Texas and the **ornate mahogany woodwork** that now graces the casino entry, lobby

INFORMATION
- ☎ 387-1896, 800-465-0711
- 🖥 www.mainstreet casino.com
- ✉ 200 N Main St
- 🚌 shuttle to/from Sam's Town & upper Strip
- ✗ Garden Court Buffet, Pullman Grille (p55)

DON'T MISS
- A self-guided tour of the antique collection
- Bronze Bank of Kuwait doors in the lobby
- Pullman Grille (p55) cigar-smoking lounge
- Monday Night Football at Triple Seven Brewpub (p59)

and the **Company Store**, which was removed from a 19th-century drugstore in Kentucky. The gorgeous **Pullman Grille** dining room was built around an ornate carved-oak fireplace and wine-storage cabinets taken from Preswick Castle in Scotland (the unique sideboard niche includes panels that depict the characters and morals of *Aesop's Fables*).

There are historic treasures at almost every turn. Pick up a free *Guide to Artifacts, Antiques & Artworks* pamphlet, which describes all the property's historic attractions, from the registration desk. Or stop for a nosh or quaff at the **Triple Seven Brewpub** (p59), which crafts its own superb suds and features live music several nights a week.

FREMONT STREET EXPERIENCE (3, D3)

A decade ago, Vegas' downtrodden Downtown had lost nearly all of its tourists to the rapidly developing Strip. It was headed downhill, fast. So,

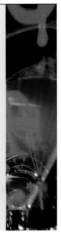

INFORMATION
- ☎ 866-373-5200
- 💻 www.vegasexperience.com
- ✉ Fremont St, btwn Main St & Las Vegas Blvd
- ℹ free light shows on the hour, every hour, 8pm-midnight
- 🚌 108, 301, 302
- 🅿 enter garage on 4th & Carson Sts; $1 for up to 5hr (validation available from most casinos)
- ✕ see p55

with no end in sight to development on The Strip, something had to be done – fast.

Always ready for a gamble, city and business boosters came up with a plan, which was realized in December 1995: a $70-million, four-block pedestrian mall topped by an arched steel canopy filled with computer-controlled lights. Five times nightly, the canopy becomes a six-minute **light-and-sound show** enhanced by 550,000 watts of wraparound sound. The latest addition is the Viva Vision super-big screen, featuring 12.5 million synchronized LEDs.

Has the newfangled mall helped business pick up Downtown? Absolutely. Although the casinos along Fremont St aren't as swanky as the megaresorts on The Strip, their proximity to one another is a real plus, and make for a vast contrast to the challenges of navigating The Strip. Parking is never a problem, there's convenient public transportation (and a monorail extension project on the horizon), and you can easily stroll between half a dozen gaming joints. What's more, the misting system built into the canopy helps to provide a welcome relief on hot days. Can you imagine that sort of lowbrow luxury at the Bellagio?

Despite all its efforts to re-fashion itself into some sort of bedazzling, family-friendly outdoor neon-lit amusement park, Downtown remains the heart and soul of old Vegas, and Fremont St retains the happy-go-lucky feel of where all the action originated.

DON'T MISS
- Free live jazz at the Golden Nugget (pp23-4)
- Big-money poker at Binion's Horseshoe (pp22-3)
- Vintage neon and the Gambling Museum at Neonopolis (p28)
- Shrimp cocktails, live piano music and congenial gold-rush vibe at the Golden Gate (p55)
- The Girls of Glitter Gulch (p67)

Sights & Activities

THRILL RIDES & AMUSEMENTS

Adventuredome (2, D2)
Circus Circus' 5-acre indoor amusement park is packed with thrills. Must-rides include the double-loop, double-corkscrew Canyon Blaster and the open-sided Rim Runner toboggan water ride. The tamer garden-variety carnival sideshow rides are popular with wee ones. Wandering clowns perform free shows throughout the day.
☎ 794-3939, 877-224-7287 🖥 www.adventuredome.com ✉ Circus Circus, 2880 Las Vegas Blvd S 💲 day pass $22/14, rides $3-6 each, kids under 33in free ⏲ varies seasonally, call for schedule

Eiffel Tower (2, C4)
Ascend in a glass elevator to the observation deck for panoramic views, with the option to dine in the Eiffel Tower Restaurant (p52) overlooking The Strip. How authentic is the half-scale tower? Gustave Eiffel's original drawings were consulted, but the 50-story replica is welded rather than riveted together. It's also fireproof and engineered to withstand a major earthquake.
☎ 946-7000, 888-266-5687 🖥 www.parislv.com ✉ Paris, 3645 Las Vegas Blvd S 💲 $9/7, under 6 free ⏲ 10-1am

GameWorks (2, C5)
Developed by Sega and Universal Studios, this high-tech arcade attracts both teens and adults. The large underground space contains a popular eatery, full bar, 75ft climbing wall, pool hall and loads of virtual-reality games. It's most crowded — and fun — at night.
☎ 432-4263 🖥 www.gameworks.com ✉ 3785 Las Vegas Blvd S 💲 free, 1/3hr unlimited play $20/27 ⏲ 10am-midnight Sun-Thu, to 2am Fri & Sat 🅿 $3

Las Vegas Cyber Speedway & Speed (2, D1)
The Speedway's Indy car simulators are so real that they excite real Formula One drivers. The faux racers are bolted to hydraulic platforms fronting 20ft wraparound screens that are scary in their realism. Speed, an electromagnetic roller-coaster, slingshots to a top speed of 70mph.
☎ 733-7223, 888-696-2121 🖥 www.nascarcafelasvegas.com ✉ Sahara, 2535 Las Vegas Blvd S 💲 Cyber Speedway $8 ($4 re-ride), Speed $13/10 ⏲ Cyber Speedway noon-9pm Sun-Thu, 11am-10pm Fri & Sat, Speed 11am-midnight, to 1am Fri & Sat

Manhattan Express (2, C5) The highlight of the ME is a heartline twist-and-dive maneuver, producing a sensation similar to that felt by a pilot during a barrel roll in a fighter plane. The rest of the four-minute ride includes stomach-dropping dipsy-dos, high-banked turns, a 540-degree spiral and good Strip views. Note that your head and shoulders may take a beating. Hold on tight and secure loose valuables in the lockers out front.
☎ 740-6969, 800-693-6763 🖥 www.nynyhotelcasino.com ✉ New York-New York, 3790 Las Vegas Blvd S 💲 $12.50 ($6 re-ride), must be 54in tall ⏲ 10am-midnight

Addicted to Speed

Richard Petty Driving Experience (1, C2)
Curious about what it's like to be in high-speed pursuit? Here's your chance to ride shotgun during a Nascar-style qualifying run. The 600-horsepower stock cars can reach speeds of up to 160mph.
☎ 643-4343, 800-237-3889 🖳 www.1800bepetty .com ✉ Las Vegas Motor Speedway, 6975 Speedway Blvd 💲 from $99 🕓 varies, call for schedule 🚌 113a

Stratosphere Tower (2, D1)
The world's highest thrill

---

rides await a whopping 110 stories above The Strip. The Big Shot straps riders into completely exposed seats that zip up and down the tower's pinnacle for 12 seconds, exerting four Gs of force. Views from the High Roller are good, but the ride is a dud – save your dough for a drink at the

Top of the World (p53). The verdict is still out on the new X Scream.
☎ 380-7777 🖳 www .stratospherehotel.com ✉ Stratosphere, 2000 Las Vegas Blvd S 💲 all rides $19, elevator $9, kids under 4 ride elevator free 🕓 10am-1am Sun-Thu, to 2am Fri & Sat

HOTEL-CASINOS

See the Highlights chapter (pp8–20) for more hotel-casinos.

Aladdin (2, C4)
Retooled to target the Asian and European jet-set, the $1.4 billion Aladdin reopened in 2000 after the 1950s original was dramatically imploded. Inside the appealing Moroccan facade are a multilevel casino, several restaurants and the impressive Desert Passage (pp37–8) shopping arcade. Upstairs, the smart London Club caters to hyper high-rollers and hosts the club, Curve (p61).
☎ 785-5555, 877-333-9474 🖳 www.aladdin casino.com ✉ 3667 Las Vegas Blvd S Ⓜ Bally's & Paris

Bally's (2, C4)
The only real theme at one of The Strip's most-cheerful

megaresorts is 'big.' Inside are a popular sports book and football field–sized casino. The epic Sterling Sunday Brunch (p46) is worth every dime, with top-shelf champagne and cracked crab legs galore. A walkway links Bally's with Paris.
☎ 739-4111, 800-634-3434 🖳 www.ballyslv .com ✉ 3645 Las Vegas Blvd S Ⓜ Bally's & Paris

Barbary Coast (2, C4)
Lavish Tiffany-styled stained glass, stately chandeliers and polished dark wood dominate this Victorian gem – only Main Street Station (p19) does turn-of-the-20th-century better. Don't miss the showpiece *Garden of Earthly Delights* stained-

glass mural on the casino's west wall. Drai's (p62) and late-night lounge acts draw a hip, party-hearty crowd.
☎ 737-7111, 888-227-2279 🖳 www.barbary coastcasino.com ✉ 3595 Las Vegas Blvd S Ⓜ Bally's & Paris

Binion's Horseshoe (3, D3)
Best known for its 'zero limit' betting policy and as host of the World Series of Poker (now shared with Harrah's), it's worth a wander to see the action in the high-stakes room and free *Honky Tonk Cowgirls* show. Binion, a savvy horse trader, once quipped 'An honest deal makes its own friends.' Although Benny's gone to the great round-up in the

Mob Oasis

The Flamingo's original owners – members of the New York mafia – shelled out an unprecedented $6 million to build the tropical gaming oasis. It was prime gangster Americana, initially managed by infamous mobster Bugsy Siegel. Soon after opening, Siegel died in a hail of bullets at his girlfriend's Beverly Hills home, the victim of a contract killing ordered by the casino's investors. In 1970, Hilton purchased the hotel, and has expanded it regularly over the years. Sadly, the Florida flamingos that used to inhabit the little islands are gone, the result of too many inconsiderate visitors who found joy in feeding them chewing gum.

sky, the Horseshoe still lives up to his motto.
☎ 384-1574, 800-622-6468 ⊒ www.binions.com ✉ 128 E Fremont St 🚌 108, 301, 302

Circus Circus (2, D2)

It's hard to miss the enormous clown-shaped marquee and the tent-shaped casino under the big top. Granted, the sprawling resort and Adventuredome (p21) complex look pretty gaudy, but there's plenty of fun to be had by all ages. Above the casino is the Midway (p29) arcade, with the cacophonous Slots-A-Fun (p28) just a stumble away.
☎ 734-0410, 800-444-2472 ⊒ www.circuscircus.com ✉ 2880 Las

Vegas Blvd S 💲 circus acts free ☽ circus acts every 30min 11am–midnight

Excalibur (2, C5)

Faux drawbridges and Arthurian legends aside, this caricature of a castle epitomizes gaudy Vegas. In a moat near the entrance, a fire-breathing dragon does mock battle with

Merlin on the hour. The dinner show, *Tournament of Kings,* is more demolition derby with hooves than flashy Vegas production.
☎ 597-7777, 877-750-5464 ⊒ www.excalibur-casino.com ✉ 3850 Las Vegas Blvd S 🚝 to/from Luxor & Mandalay Bay

Flamingo (2, C4)

In 1946, the Flamingo was the talk of the town. Today, it isn't quite what it was back when its janitorial staff wore tuxedos, but its magnificent gardens, 15 acres of pools, waterfalls and waterways are still a sight to behold. Stop by during happy hour (4pm to 7pm) at the hotel's bars and restaurants.
☎ 733-3111, 800-732-2111 ⊒ www.flamingolv.com ✉ 3555 Las Vegas Blvd S Ⓜ Flamingo & Caesars

Golden Nugget (3, D3)

The Nugget has set the Downtown benchmark for total extravagance since opening in 1946. Thanks to an injection of chutzpah by Fox's *Casino* reality show stars Tim and Tom, it's still at the top of its class. The luxurious rooms are good

The First Carpet Joint

The legendary Fremont has been packing 'em in since 1956, when it opened as Downtown's first high-rise. Separating it from the pack was its wall-to-wall carpeting – all the nearby casinos had sawdust-covered floors. It was here, too, that lounge singer Wayne Newton launched his long-standing career. With the exception of its superb restaurants, the Fremont has today slipped into mediocrity.

value and no brass or cut glass was spared in the Victorian casino. Don't miss the gigantic 61lb Hand of Faith nugget in the lobby. ☎ 385-7111, 800-846-5336 🖳 www.golden nugget.com ✉ 129 E Fremont St 🚌 108, 301, 302

Hard Rock Hotel & Casino (2, D4)

The Hard Rock is home to one of the world's most impressive collections of rock 'n' roll memorabilia. The complex consists of an unremarkable Hard Rock Cafe and an über-trendy hotel-casino. Inside, the Joint concert hall (p63),

the happening Center Bar and the nightclub Body English (p61) attract a done-up, sex-charged crowd. ☎ 693-5000, 800-473-7625 🖳 www.hrhvegas .com ✉ 4455 Paradise Rd 🚌 108, free Strip shuttle 10am-7pm

---

A Real Class Joint

In 1958, the new $10-million Stardust was a 'real class joint,' as the mobsters used to say. With 1065 rooms, it was also the world's largest resort complex. The Dunes introduced bare-breasted showgirls to Vegas with *Minsky Goes to Paris* in 1957, but the Stardust countered by importing real French showgirls for *Lido de Paris*. Today, the Stardust's entertainment consists chiefly of a washed-up Wayne Newton.

Cool Pools

Vegas is home to some truly spectacular aquatic hangouts, which are open to guests during spring and summer. The coolest ones are the Garden of the Gods at Caesars Palace (p10), Mandalay Bay's (p11) wave pool and clothing-optional Moorea Beach Club, the huge complex at the Tropicana (p26), the lagoon at the Mirage (p14) and the hip Beach Club at the Hard Rock (p24), which features swim-up blackjack.

Harrah's (2, C3)

Everywhere you look there's something playfully suggestive of carnival or Mardi Gras, like the enormous backlit mural over the main entrance featuring Sin City's entertainment legends. Inside, one of the largest and brightest casinos in town is usually packed, as is the popular lounge. ☎ 369-5000, 800-392-9002 🖳 www.harrahs .com ✉ 3475 Las Vegas Blvd S Ⓜ Harrah's & Imperial Palace

Imperial Palace (2, C4)

Though the pagoda facade is a bit hokey, the Oriental theme at this popular low-limit casino is tastefully done. Plus, dealers in the casino do celebrity impersonations. Attractions include an impressive auto collection (p27) and The Strip's *Legends in Concert*, the best celebrity impersonator show. ☎ 731-3311, 800-634-6441 🖳 www.imperial palace.com ✉ 3535 Las Vegas Blvd S Ⓜ Paris & Imperial Palace

Las Vegas Hilton (2, E2)

Thanks to its proximity to the convention center the Hilton is popular with

The Spa Who Loved Me

Most spas on The Strip are reserved for registered hotel guests on weekends, but are often open to nonguests during the week. Day-use fees are $20 to $35; treatments run from $100 to $175 per hour.

Spa Bellagio (p8) Perfect for groups of friends. Newly expanded, this is the pinnacle of Euro-style pampering.

Venetian's Canyon Ranch SpaClub (p9) Popular with couples for side-by-side treatments. Offers rhythmic Abhyanga massage and a 40-ft rock-climbing wall.

Palms' Amp Spa (p25) Ultra-soft 'cashwear' robes, stone massage and a celebrity stylist – what are you waiting for?

Luxor's Oasis Spa (p18) Open 24/7. Enough said.

Jennifer L Leo

business travelers. The classy casino doesn't attract many glassy-eyed low-rollers, but it does have the sci-fi Star Trek motion-simulator ride. Mature wheelers and dealers often find this the best place in town to mix business with pleasure.
☎ 732-5111, 888-732-7117 🖳 www.lvhilton.com ✉ 3000 Paradise Rd Ⓜ Hilton

What's Free?

When you're down to the felt (your last dime), don't despair. There's free entertainment at Circus Circus (p23), Rio's Masquerade Show in the Sky (pp25–6), the Sirens of TI (p12), Excalibur's magic acts (p23), Caesars Forum Shops animatronic shows (p38), Bellagio's fountains (p8), MGM Grand's lion habitat (p29) and Mirage's tiger habitat and faux volcano (p14).

Join in the fun at the Masquerade Show in the Sky.

Monte Carlo (2, C5)

A joint venture between the owners of Bellagio and Mandalay Bay, the Monte Carlo aims for the European elegance of the former and the entertainment luster of the latter. The casino is bustling and spacious but otherwise the property is a poor man's Caesars Palace. For entertainment, there's master magician Lance Burton, many critic's pick for Vegas' best illusionist.
☎ 730-7777, 888-529-4828 🖳 www.montecarlo.com ✉ 3770 Las Vegas Blvd S 🚃 to/from Bellagio

Palms (2, A4)

Still basking in MTV's *Real World* glow, the Palms attracts a younger, mostly local crowd. Although there's no coherent theme, no expense seems to have been spared. There's an unpretentious mix of bars and restaurants, a spa and salon, a 14-screen cinema, an IMAX theater, a 1200-seat showroom and a big casino. Topping it all off (literally) is the trendy ghostbar (p59).
☎ 942-7777, 866-725-6773 🖳 www.palms.com ✉ 4321 W Flamingo Rd 🚌 202

Rio (2, B4)

Forget carnival, the festive Rio is positioning itself as bachelorette headquarters with its new Chippendales' nightlife complex (p67). There's a good mix of restaurants and buffets, shopping and gaming choices, plus loads of free entertainment. The free *Masquerade Show*

in the Sky is enough of a spectacle to make Hunter S Thompson blush (or reach for his shotgun).
☎ 777-7777, 800-752-9746 🖥 www.playrio.com ✉ 3700 W Flamingo Rd 🚌 202, free Strip shuttle

Sahara (2, D1)
Thanks to a $100 million face-lift, the Moroccan-themed Sahara is one of the few old-Vegas carpet joints that have survived the megaresort onslaught. The Arabian nights theme continues inside the casino. Most compelling, perhaps, are the NASCAR Cafe's thrill rides at the Cyber Speedway (p21).
☎ 737-2111, 888-696-2121 🖥 www.saharavegas.com ✉ 2535 Las Vegas Blvd S Ⓜ Sahara

Stardust (2, D2)
Stuck in no-man's-land, the Stardust has stuck to its Rat Pack roots and continues to lure fans of bygone Vegas. You gotta love the landmark 188ft starry sign, which is cast in nearly every Hollywood-movie establishing shot of Vegas. After Wynn Las Vegas (p72) opens across the way, the 'dust' will be a likely implosion candidate.
☎ 732-6111, 866-642-3120 🖥 www.stardustlv.com ✉ 3000 Las Vegas Blvd S

Tropicana (2, C5)
Built in 1957, the Trop has had nearly half a century to lose its luster, but thanks to a few lifts and tucks, it's

Top Five Poker Hotspots

- For ultra high-limit stakes, the Bellagio (p8) is the biggest and best game in town. Lower-limit tables cater to up-and-comers.
- The Mirage (p14) has 31 tables devoted to varying limits of Seven Card Stud, Texas Hold 'em, Omaha Eight and more.
- Best known for hosting Bravo's *Celebrity Poker Showdown,* the Palms (p25) hosts no-limit Texas Hold 'em 24/7.
- The Golden Nugget (pp23–4) boasts a nonsmoking room and is a favorite of high-stakes players.
- Binion's Horseshoe (pp22–3), the original home of the World Series of Poker, is old school all the way

Jennifer L Leo

looking better than ever. There's a festive Caribbean village, exotic birds in the Wildlife Walk and a Polynesian longhouse that hosts Hawaiian musicians. Entertainment options include swim-up blackjack, the long-running *Folies Bergére* (p65), the Comedy Stop (p63) and the Casino Legends Hall of Fame (p28).
☎ 739-2222, 888-826-8767 🖥 www.tropicanalv.com ✉ 3801 Las Vegas Blvd S Ⓜ MGM

If I Was a Gambling Man…

Loath to lay your money on the table without a clue? Aladdin (p22), Barbary Coast (p22), Circus Circus (p23), Excalibur (p23) and New York–New York (p16) offer informal gambling lessons on weekday mornings. Contact the front desk or ask the main cage for details.

ART GALLERIES & MUSEUMS

Bellagio Gallery of Fine Art (2, C4)

Since Steve Wynn sold his baby to MGM for $6.4 billion, the Bellagio hasn't been blessed with the same world-class art, but it still hosts unique traveling shows such as the Monet spectacular, *Claude Monet: Masterworks from the Museum of Fine Arts, Boston*. ☎ 693-7871, 877-957-9777 🖳 www.bellagio.com ✉ Bellagio, 3600 Las Vegas Blvd S 💲 $15/12 🕐 9am-9pm

Guggenheim Hermitage Museum (2, C3)

A partnership with Russia's State Hermitage Museum of St Petersburg ensures the masterpieces keep on coming at this austere gallery. The focus of the Guggenheim Hermitage's vast and impressive collection is impressionism, postimpressionism and early modernism. ☎ 414-2440, 866-484-4849 🖳 www.guggenheimlasvegas.org

✉ Venetian, Lobby level, 3355 Las Vegas Blvd S 💲 $15/7-11, under 6 free 🕐 9:30am-8:30pm

Imperial Palace Auto Collection (2, C4)

Car buffs could easily pass an entire day viewing one of the world's largest privately owned auto collections. Among the wonderful vehicles on hand (all of which are for sale): Steve McQueen's 1923 Indian Big Chief; Tom Jones' 1981 Mercedes-Benz 500 SEL sedan and more Rolls-Royces than you can toss a chauffeur at. ☎ 731-3311 🖳 www.autocollections.com ✉ Imperial Palace, 5th fl, 3535 Las Vegas Blvd S 💲 $7, free coupons available on website 🕐 9:30am-9:30pm Ⓜ Harrah's & Imperial Palace

King Tut Museum (2, C6)

Exquisite reproductions of the artifacts discovered by English archaeologist Howard Carter on his apocryphal descent into the fabled tomb of an obscure Egyptian dynasty are explained during a 15-minute, self-guided audio tour. ☎ 262-4000 🖳 www.luxor.com ✉ Luxor, 3900 Las Vegas Blvd S 💲 $5 🕐 9am-midnight 🚋 to/from Excalibur & Mandalay Bay

Marjorie Barrick Museum of Natural History (2, E4)

UNLV's hidden cultural gem is an anthropological treasure trove. Exhibits range from a Southwestern herpitarium (with live feedings of native iguanas and gila monsters) and early Vegas history to modern art galleries and a Xeriscape desert garden. ☎ 895-3381 🖳 http://hrcweb.nevada.edu/museum/index.html ✉ UNLV, cnr Swenson St & Harmon Ave 💲 free 🕐 8am-4:45pm Mon-Fri, 10am-2pm Sat 🚌 108 🅿 metered parking

O'Shea's Magic & Movie Hall of Fame (2, C3)

Abracadabra: low-rolling O'Shea's is home to one of the world's top magic museums. On display are Hollywood memorabilia, props from famous magicians and videos of Houdini in action. Live comedy acts and a free drink round out the entertaining package. ☎ 792-9550 ✉ O'Shea's Casino, 2nd fl, 3555 Las Vegas Blvd S 💲 $5 🕐 1-10pm Tue-Sun, shows 4:30pm & 8:30pm

Wynn Collection (2, C3)

Casino mogul Steve Wynn's heavyweight fine art collection – with a dozen original works by Cézanne, Van Gogh, Matisse, Gauguin, Picasso and Warhol – will grace the walls of Wynn Las Vegas (p72) after it opens in April 2005. ☎ 770-7000, 877-770-7077 🖳 www.wynnlasvegas.com ✉ Wynn Las Vegas, 3145 Las Vegas Blvd S

Culture in Sin City

QUIRKY LAS VEGAS

Casino Legends Hall of Fame (2, C5)

The world's largest gambling museum stockpiles 15,000 pieces of gaming and celebrity memorabilia. Don't miss the video about famous hotel implosions – a quirky bit of local lore. Join the Tropicana's Winners Club for free admission coupons.

☎ 739-2222 🖳 www.tropicanalv.com ✉ Tropicana, 3801 Las Vegas Blvd S 💲 $7/6 🕑 9am-9pm Ⓜ MGM Grand

Elvis-A-Rama Museum (2, C3)

The King may have left the building, but his impersonators and the largest private collection of his memorabilia are still very much in the house. It's gaudy, cheesy and over-the-top, but then so was the man himself.

☎ 309-7200 🖳 www.elvisarama.com ✉ 3401 Industrial Rd 💲 admission $15-28 🕑 10am-8pm 🚌 free Strip shuttle, call for pick-up

Liberace Museum (1, B4)

For connoisseurs of over-the-top extravagance, this place is a must-do. The home of 'Mr Showmanship' houses the most flamboyant art cars, outrageous costumes and ornate pianos you'll ever see. There's a hand-painted Pleyel, on which Chopin played; a red, white and blue Rolls-Royce convertible; and a wardrobe exhibit full of feathered capes and million-dollar furs, darling.

☎ 798-5595 🖳 www.liberace.org ✉ 1775 E Tropicana Ave 💲 $12/8 🕑 10am-5pm Mon-Sat, 1-5pm Sun 🚌 201, free Strip shuttle, call for pick-up

Neon Museum (3, D3)

Plaques tell the story of each sign at this alfresco assemblage of vintage neon. Sparkling genie lamps, glowing martini glasses and 1940s motel marquees brighten up this otherwise bleak slice of Downtown. Look for the flashy 40ft-tall chap on horseback.

☎ 387-6366 🖳 www.neonmuseum.org ✉ cnr Fremont & 3rd Sts 💲 free 🕑 24/7/365 🚌 108, 301, 302 Ⓟ at Neonopolis

Slots-A-Fun (2, D2)

For cheap drinks, cheap eats and cheap thrills, it's tough to beat this low-brow dive. Grab a coupon book from neighboring Circus Circus (p23), a few 75¢ beers and $1 half-pound hot dogs. Then kick back, relax and enjoy the laughable lounge acts.

☎ 734-0410 ✉ 2890 Las Vegas Blvd S 💲 free 🕑 24/7/365 🚌 301, 302 Ⓟ free at Circus Circus

Viva Las Vegas Wedding Chapel (3, C5)

Even if you're not contemplating tying the knot, it's worth a peek inside to see if anyone is getting married – the public is welcome and ceremonies are broadcast live online. The themed hotel rooms (p73) are fun for non-honeymooners too. Call to check the current wedding schedule.

☎ 384-0771, 800-574-4450 🖳 www.vivalasvegasweddings.com ✉ 1205 Las Vegas Blvd S 💲 free 🚌 108

Cheesy, Cheesy: Vegas, Baby!

Enjoy a wacky day Vegas style:

- Trawl The Strip for Elvis impersonators and the best lounge acts (p63) at 3am
- Fill up on cheap fun with the best coupon books in town at Slots-a-Fun (p28)
- Drop a few in the slots while trapeze acts whiz overhead at Circus Circus (p23)
- Indulge after-hours with a treatment or full-body tanning at Luxor's 24hr Oasis Spa (p18)
- Do your best celebrity impersonation: get married and divorced within 24-hour, just like Britney Spears!

LAS VEGAS FOR CHILDREN

Now that sin is in again, few places in Vegas bill themselves as family-friendly. State law prohibits people under 21 from loitering in gaming areas and The Strip has a selectively enforced curfew for youth under 18 after 9pm. The only megaresorts that cater to children are Circus Circus (p23) and Excalibur (p23), and some actively discourage kids by prohibiting strollers. That said, there's still plenty to do with the wee ones. Beyond the arcades and rides, teenagers will likely be bored out of their minds. Look for the 🏃 icon in the book to identify kid-friendly options.

Circus Circus Midway (2, D2)

Has free circus performances daily on center stage. Grab a seat; there's no admission charge or reserved seating. Nearby are loads of arcades with both video and old-fashioned carnival games.
☎ 734-0410, 800-444-2472 🖥 www.circus circus.com ✉ Circus Circus, 2880 Las Vegas Blvd S 💲 free ⏰ 11am-midnight, shows every 30min

Court Jesters Stage (2, C5)

A free medieval extravaganza with musicians playing period instruments and magicians performing feats that medieval alchemists never would have imagined possible. There are also jugglers and puppeteers.
☎ 597-7777, 800-937-7777 🖥 www.excalibur-casino.com ✉ Excalibur, 3050 Las Vegas Blvd S 💲 free ⏰ 10am-10pm Mon-Thu, 10am-1am Fri & Sat, shows every 30min

Las Vegas Natural History Museum (3, E2)

There's heaps for the kids to do at this museum, which is divided into five themed rooms. Highlights include the aquariums, native Nevada wildlife taxidermy, fossils and animatronic tyrannosauruses, and the hands-on science center.
☎ 384-3466 🖥 www .lvnhm.org ✉ 900 N Las Vegas Blvd 💲 $6/3, children under 3 free ⏰ 9am-4pm 🚌 113

MGM Grand Lion Habitat (2, C5)

This multilevel enclosure showcases up to six adult lions daily. MGM owns eight of the magnificent felines, but only two are in the enclosure. Don't miss the see-through walkway tunnel, where the big cats roam around onlookers.
☎ 891-1111 🖥 www .mgmgrand.com ✉ MGM, 3799 Las Vegas Blvd S 💲 free ⏰ 11am-10pm MGM Grand

Siegfried & Roy's Secret Garden & Dolphin Habitat (2, C3)

The Mirage's tropical garden features lions, tigers, jaguars and an elephant. The cats are often napping; late afternoon is the best chance to see them frolicking. Up-close-and-personal Atlantic bottlenose-dolphin interactions and viewing areas are the highlights of the aquarium.
☎ 791-7188 🖥 www .mirage.com ✉ Mirage, 3400 Las Vegas Blvd S 💲 $12, under 10 free ⏰ 11am-7pm Mon-Fri, 10am-7pm Sat & Sun

Babysitting & Child Care

The Gold Coast (p74), MGM Grand (p72) and Orleans (p74) have on-site child-care centers. Or check out agencies such as **Around the Clock Childcare** (☎ 365-1040, 800-798-6768), which charges $52 per child for a four-hour minimum plus $11 for each additional hour. Employees have been fingerprinted by police and background-checked by the FBI.

Out & About

WALKING TOURS
Around the World in Half a Day

Inside the **Venetian** (**1**; p9), grab a gondola or stroll through the Grand Canal Shoppes (p38) to St Mark's Square. Cross The Strip on the walkway to **Treasure Island** (T1; **2**; p12). If it's after 7pm, check out the free *Sirens of TI* show in Sirens' Cove. From TI, hop on a tram to the **Mirage** (**3**; p14) and ogle the faux volcano, white tigers and Siegfried & Roy's Secret Garden (p29). Saunter south along The Strip to the **Forum Shops** (**4**; p38)

Mime your way in the Venetian

and **Caesars Palace** (**5**; p10). Cross Flamingo Rd via a skyway to the **Bellagio** (**6**; p8), where lush floral displays and world-class window shopping await. Break for a gamble or nosh at a casino-side café.

Cross The Strip and wend your way through **Bally's** (**7**; p22) via the cobblestone Rue de la Paix shopping arcade (p39) to **Paris** (**8**; p15) for a ride up the Eiffel Tower (p21). Hop on the monorail to the imposing **MGM Grand** (**9**; p13). Visit the lion habitat and glam gaming area, then follow the walkway to **New York-New York** (**10**; p16). Pay your respects at the 9/11 memorial then wander Greenwich Village and ride the Manhattan Express (p21). Cross the skyway to the **Excalibur** (**11**; p23) then ride the tram to **Mandalay Bay** (**12**; p11). Top off your transglobal journey with a tram ride back up to the **Luxor** (**13**; p18) with its pyramid and King Tut's tomb.

---

distance 2.5mi **duration** 4-5hr
▶ **start** 🚌 Venetian's bus stop
● **end** 🚋 Luxor's tram stop

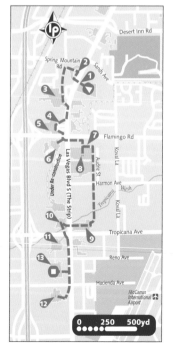

Stripside Amusements – Thrills & Spills

At the **Stratosphere** (**1**; p17) buy a combo ticket to ride the USA's fastest elevators to the Top of the World (p53) then head for the Big Shot and High Roller rides (p22). Decompress with a southward jaunt along The Strip to the **Sahara** (**2**; p26) before hopping aboard Speed (p21) or racing nearly full-size, very realistic stock cars at the Cyber Speedway (p21). Stroll The Strip south to **Circus Circus** (**3**; p23). Check out the rides at Adventuredome (p21) then stop for a snack at **Slots-A-Fun** (**4**; p28).

Feel the Speed

Hail a taxi, trolley or bus down The Strip to the **Showcase Mall** (**5**; p39) to experience the virtual-reality rides at the high-tech Game Works arcade (p21). Save some stamina for the walk through **MGM Grand** (**6**; p13) to the sky-bridge across The Strip to **New York-New York** (**7**; p16), where the Coney Island Emporium arcade and exhilarating Manhattan Express (p21) roller coaster await. Stop for a snack in Little Italy or a nibble in Greenwich Village before taking the skybridge to the **Excalibur** (**8**; p23) to catch the tram to the **Luxor** (**9**; p18) via Mandalay Bay. Inside the pyramid, make a beeline for the Games of the Gods arcade to test-drive some of the latest and greatest interactive amusements.

distance 3.5mi **duration** 4-5hr
▶ **start** 🚌 Stratosphere bus/trolley stop
⏺ **end** 🚌 Luxor bus/trolley stop

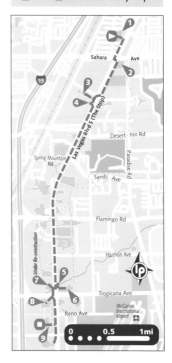

Spin the night away at Adventuredome

Historic Downtown – Naked City & Glitter Gulch

From The Strip, hail a taxi (p84) or catch CAT bus 301 or 302 bus (p84) up Main St through the downtrodden Naked City district – so named for the proliferation of strip clubs – to the Downtown Transportation Center. Follow Stewart Ave west to **Main Street Station** (**1**; p19) and take the self-guided tour of architectural artifacts, then head south down Main St to the Plaza Hotel. Cross over to pedestrian-only Fremont St and sidle into the **Golden Gate** (**2**; p55), where you can test your luck in the

cozy casino. Try to imagine what life was like here in 1905 when the Union Pacific Railroad auctioned off dusty lots in what was then known as Ragtown. Continue through the heart of **Glitter Gulch** (**3**), where Vegas' original Strip has been madeover and renamed as the Fremont Street Experience (p20). Try to envision this corridor before the dancing lights overshadowed the neon.

Step inside the classy **Golden Nugget** (**4**; pp23–4) for a pick-me-up and to ogle the gigantic Hand of Faith. Cross over to **Binion's Horseshoe** (**5**; pp22–3) to check out the action in the high-stakes poker room. Continue on down to 3rd St and the **Neon Museum** (**6**; p28), an alfresco assemblage of vintage signs. **Neonopolis** (**7**; p39) also has a noteworthy collection of vintage neon on display, plus a new gambling museum, Lost Vegas (p43).

Fremont Street Experience

distance 1mi **duration** 1-2hr
- ▶ **start** 🚌 Downtown Transportation Center
- ● **end** 🚌 CAT Las Vegas Blvd bus depot

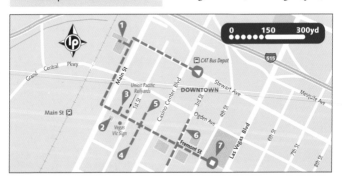

DAY TRIPS
Hoover Dam & Lake Mead   (4, B2)

One of the world's tallest diversions, **Hoover Dam** (726ft) has a striking beauty, with its imposing, graceful concrete curve filling a dramatic red-rock canyon, backed by the brilliant blue waters of **Lake Mead**. Its

simple form and art deco embellishments sit beautifully within the stark landscape. Finished in 1936, the dam was a rare public works project completed two years ahead of schedule and $14 million under budget, at a total cost of $165 million. When you tire of admiring the view and pretending to jump the railing (no terrorist jokes, please – that sort of thing is taken *very* seriously around here) make a beeline for the refrigerated gift shop, where you can pick up unique, all-American novelties for your loved ones: 'Dam Proud to Be An American' bumper stickers; super-coolio mesh hats; Hoover Dam–shaped ceramic mugs and refrigerator magnets – you name it, bub.

Flood control, irrigation, electricity and a regulated water supply to the city were the purposes of the dam's construction, and they remain its primary functions. The lower Colorado River irrigates a million acres of land in the USA and half a million in Mexico; it slakes the thirst of 25 million people and generates four billion kilowatt hours a year.

The usual **scenic drive** follows North Shore Rd, which starts near the **visitor center** and leads up to the fine **Lost City Museum** in Overton and scenic **Valley of Fire State Park**.

If driving, ditch your vehicle in the parking lot before you reach the dam. **Bus tours** (left) from Vegas are a good deal and guarantee a ticket for the dam tour.

INFORMATION
26mi southeast of Las Vegas

- From The Strip (30min-1hr): Flamingo Rd (SR 592) east to I-515/Hwy 93/95; at Boulder City, take Hwy 93 east
- ☎ 702-293-8907
- 🖳 www.nps.gov/lame, www.usbr.gov/lc/hooverdam
- $ parking $5 per vehicle, tours $10 per person
- 🕐 visitor centers 8:30am-4:30pm, dam tours 9am-5pm
- ℹ Alan Bible Visitor Center (☎ 293-8990; Hwy 93), Hoover Dam Visitor Center (☎ 294-3524; Hwy 93)
- 🗶 Snacketeria at Nevada spillway

Grand Canyon (4, F2)

Grand Canyon National Park (☎ 928-638-7888; www.nps.gov/grca) is arguably the USA's best-known natural attraction. At 277 miles long, roughly 10 miles wide and 1 mile deep, the canyon is an incredible spectacle of Technicolor rock strata.

The canyon's many peaks and buttes and its meandering rims give access to fantastic views. Descending into the canyon on **hiking trails** offers the best sense of the breathtaking variety in the landscape, wildlife and climate. Popular **flightseeing day trips** from Las Vegas (often combined with flyovers of Hoover Dam and Lake Mead, and a ground tour of the South Rim) provide short-stay visitors with a good introduction to this stunning hole in the ground.

Although the rims are only 10 miles apart as the crow flies, it's a 215-mile, five-hour drive on narrow roads between the North and South Rim visitor centers. Though the South Rim is the most visited, the **North Rim** is actually a little closer to Las Vegas, and it's a lot closer to Utah's **Zion** and **Bryce Canyon National Parks**. If you want to see more than just the Grand Canyon on your own, consider skipping the congested South Rim.

Reputable Vegas–based flightseeing operators include **Air Vegas** (☎ 736-3599, 800-255-7474; www.airvegas.com), **Grand Canyon Tour Company** (☎ 655-6060, 800-222-6966; www.grandcanyontourcompany.com) and **Scenic Airlines** (☎ 638-3300, 800-634-6801; www.scenic.com). Rates for hour-long air tours start at around $100 per person; day-long air/ground combos run $200 to $250 per person, and premier helicopter tours landing on the canyon's floor fetch $300 per person.

INFORMATION

278mi east of Las Vegas

- 🚌 From The Strip (5-6hr): E Tropicana Ave east to I-515 south; I-515 south to Hwy 93; Hwy 93 south to I-40 east to Hwy 64; Hwy 64 north 60mi to the South Rim Visitor Center at Grand Canyon Village; North Rim is 215mi (about 4½hr) from the South Rim by car
- ☎ 928-638-7888
- 🖥 www.nps.gov/grca
- 💲 $20 per vehicle (good for seven days)
- 🕐 Canyon View Information Plaza 8am-5pm, Desert View Information Center 9am-6pm, North Rim Visitor Center 8am-6pm mid-May –mid-Oct
- ℹ South Rim entrance facilities 🕐 24/7/365; North Rim visitor services and facilities 🕐 mid-May–mid-Oct
- 🍽 South Rim: El Tovar Dining Room, Maswik Cafeteria, Hermits Rest Snack Bar; North Rim: Grand Canyon Lodge Dining Room

ORGANIZED TOURS

Most tours appeal to seniors who prefer to leave the driving to others. It's easy enough to tour The Strip on your own via monorail, taxi, trolley, bus or rental car, but Hoover Dam package deals can save a lot of ticketing headaches and adventure outfitters can ease logistic hassles. Free hotel pick-up and drop-off from The Strip are included in most rates. Check online for frequent promotions.

Black Canyon River Adventures Take a 12-mile motor-assisted journey down the Colorado River. Boats launch from the base of Hoover Dam (p33) and visit several hot springs en route to Willow Beach Marina.
☎ 294-1414, 800-455-3490 🖳 www.black canyonadventures.com ✉ Hacienda Hotel, Boulder City $ $73/45 plus $106 transportation from Las Vegas

Escape Adventures Escape the neon jungle for a single-track mountain-bike, road-bike or hiking tour of stunning Red Rock Canyon. The packages include free hotel transfers.
☎ 596-2953, 800-596-2953 🖳 www.escape adventures.com $ half/fullday from $89/149

Gray Line Tours The granddaddy of group sightseeing runs the most-popular night-time city tour, which combines buses and short walks and lasts five hours. Stops include Bellagio's fountains, the Casino Legends Museum and the Fremont Street Experience.
☎ 735-4947, 800-634-6579 🖳 www.grayline .com $ $40 🕑 6:30pm

Red Rock Canyon, just 20 miles west of The Strip

Rocky Trails Adventure Tours This one-stop shop for outdoor adventure tours arranges everything from guided kayak floats below Hoover Dam and glider soaring rides to off-road ATV tours and 4WD ghost-town explorations.
☎ 869-9991, 888-846-4747 🖳 www.adventure lasvegas.com $ $99-499 🕑 reservations 24/7

Papillon Grand Canyon Helicopters Vegas' oldest helicopter-flightseeing outfitter does luxury tours all over the Southwest. Its half-hour Neon Nights jetcopter flyover of The Strip and dinner flight package are the most-notable offerings.
☎ 736-7243, 888-635-7272 🖳 www.papillon .com $ $55-75 with dinner $112-142 🕑 departs 6-9pm

Pink Jeep Tours Offers intimate off-road adventure alternatives to the traditional bus tour. On the menu are the Valley of Fire, Mt Charleston, Red Rock Canyon, Hoover Dam and Eldorado Canyon. The Ultimate Grand Canyon Combo includes brief helicopter and pontoon boat rides.
☎ 895-6777, 888-900-4480 🖳 www.pinkjeep lasvegas.com $ half day $69-99, full day $175-305

Shopping

Las Vegas is a shopper's paradise. Consumption is as conspicuous as dancing fountains in the middle of the desert. Upscale international haute purveyors cater to the cashed-up – you can find almost anything (name brand, at least) that you'd find in London or Los Angeles. Plus a few unique high-roller items not likely to be sold anytime soon, like Ginger Rogers' 7.02 carat marquis diamond engagement ring, and the world's largest carved emerald, both on display in Fred Leighton at the Bellagio (p39).

Stroll the Desert Passage

The Las Vegas Valley has over 30 million sq ft of retail space, and that staggering figure is growing as fast as the region's thirst for water. Vegas, however, isn't like Istanbul, where 80% of visitors purchase a handmade carpet before heading home. Rather, it's a place where you can buy almost anything, if you have deep pockets. And because so much is sold to visitors, most merchants happily arrange to have your newfound goodies shipped home.

Shopping Areas

The Strip is the focus of the shopping action, with upscale boutiques concentrated in the newer resorts fronting the southern half. **Downtown** and the **Westside** are the places to cruise for wigs, naughty adult goods and trashy lingerie. On the **Eastside** near UNLV, Maryland Parkway is chock-a-block with hip shops catering to the college crowd. Malls dominate the scene but upscale specialty shops at megaresorts stay open late. Trendy one-off boutiques are scarce, but are popping up on the fringes of The Strip.

Cruise Downtown for desert antiques

DEPARTMENT STORES & SHOPPING CENTERS

Bally's Avenue Shoppes (2, C4) Bally's polished subterranean promenade is notable for the good-natured gags and in-store magicians at Houdini's Magic Shop and signature magnets at the Las Vegas Experience souvenir shop. ☎ 739-4111 ✉ Bally's, 3645 Las Vegas Blvd S ☼ 9am-11pm Ⓜ Bally's & Paris

More Bling Bling Than Ding Ding

Name designers are as common as casinos. Witness **Prada** (☎ 866-6886) at Bellagio; **Louis Vuitton** at the Forum Shops (☎ 732-1227) and Fashion Show Mall (☎ 731-9860); **Chanel** (☎ 765-5505) at Via Bellagio; **Versace** (☎ 792-9372) at Caesars Forum; **Jimmy Choo** (☎ 733-1802) at Grand Canal Shoppes; **Tiffany** (☎ 697-5400) at Bellagio and **Rolex** (☎ 733-0003) at Fashion Show Mall. Most mega-resorts have jewelry stores with lovely adornments, like **Cartier** (☎ 733-6652) at Caesars Palace.

Boulevard Mall (2,F3) Nevada's second-largest mall – it was recently trumped by the Fashion Show Mall – is only a few minutes east of The Strip. What it lacks in quality it makes up for in quantity. Among the 170 tenants are Gap, Radio Shack and Victoria's Secret. Five department stores (Dillard's, JC Penney, Macy's, Marshall's and Sears) and an elaborate food court round out the middle-class line-up. ☎ 732-8949 ✉ 3528 Maryland Parkway ☼ 10am-9pm Mon-Sat, 11am-6pm Sun 🚌 109, 110, 112

Desert Passage (2, C4) Aladdin's upscale North African–themed marketplace has 130 retailers and a dozen restaurants, plus a

Blue Light Specials: Shop Til' You Pop

Brand-name bargain hunters can 'buy direct' at the following outlet malls:

Las Vegas Outlet Center (1, B4; ☎ 896-5599; 7400 S Las Vegas Blvd; ☼ 10am-10pm Mon-Sat, 10am-9pm Sun) A five-minute drive south of the airport, and with 130 stores, including lots of houseware (Dansk, Corning-Revere, Off 5th) and shoe shops (Famous Footwear, Nine West, Reebok). For the kiddies, there's a full-size carousel.

Fashion Outlet Mall (1, A6 ; ☎ 874-1400, 888-424-6898; 32100 S Las Vegas Blvd; ☼ 10am-8pm) Forty-five minutes southwest of Vegas , off I-15 exit 1 in Primm, near the Nevada/California state line. There's a good mix of 100 high-end (Coach, Escada, Versace, Williams Sonoma, Neiman Marcus' Last Call) and everyday (Banana Republic, Gap, Old Navy, Nautica, Sketchers) brands. If you're not driving, it's accessible from The Strip via a shopper shuttle ($13) that departs daily from MGM Grand, Aladdin's Desert Passage and New York-New York. Call the toll-free number for shuttle reservations.

Las Vegas Premium Outlets (3, B4; ☎ 474-7500; 875 S Grand Central Pkwy; ☼ 10am-10pm Mon-Sat, 10am-9pm Sun) The most upscale of Vegas' outlets features 120 high-end names like Armani Exchange, Coach, Dolce & Gabbana, Guess, Kenneth Cole and Polo Ralph Lauren. There's also a few mid-range options, like Eddie Bauer and Levi's. Beyond the shops, there's a decent food court and plenty of pleasant outdoor seating – but you'll want to spend most of your time inside in the air-con. The Downtown Shoppers Express shuttle serves the mall every 20 minutes from 10am until 5pm.

Wynn's Fantasyland

Steve Wynn's new eponymous blockbuster resort (open April 2005) will contain art galleries and 75,000 sq ft leased to high-end retailers like Chanel, Louis Vuitton, Cartier and Jean-Paul Gaultier. After you hit the jackpot, take a test drive at the Ferarri and Maserati dealerships.

rainy harbor and scads of wandering street performers. The emphasis is on jewelry, gifts and women's apparel. Cargo bikes await to transport baggage-laden shoppers to the remote parking garage.
☎ 736-7114 💻 www .desertpassage.com ✉ Aladdin, 3663 Las Vegas Blvd S 🕙 10am-10pm Sun-Thu, to midnight Fri & Sat Ⓜ Bally's & Paris

Fashion Show Mall (2, C3)
Unique shops are sparse at Nevada's biggest and flashiest – and The Strip's only – mall, but at least it's centrally located. There are 250 storefronts, plus Bloomingdale's, Dillard's, Neiman Marcus, Nordstrom, Saks Fifth Avenue, Robinsons-May and Macy's department stores. Models hit the runway afternoons Wednesday to Sunday. It has a good food court. Look for The Cloud (a multimedia canopy) out front.
☎ 369-0704 💻 www .thefashionshow.com ✉ 3200 Las Vegas Blvd S 🕙 10am-9pm Mon-Fri, 10am-7pm Sat, noon-6pm Sun

Forum Shops (2, C4)
At the nation's profitable consumer playground Frank-lins fly out of Fendi bags faster than in high-roller casinos. Caesars' fanciful re-creation of an ancient Roman market houses 150 designer emporia, including one-name catwalk wonders like Armani, Escada, Versace, Fendi and MaxMara. Animatronic shows and a 50,000-gallon aquarium boost the entertainment quotient. Don't miss the new spiral escalator.
☎ 893-4800 💻 www .shopcaesars.com ✉ Caesars Palace, 3500 Las Vegas Blvd S 🕙 10am-11pm Sun-Thu, to midnight Fri & Sat Ⓜ Flamingo & Caesars

Grand Canal Shoppes (2, C3)
Living statues and mezzo-sopranos lurk among 75 upscale shops and art galleries at this indoor mall. Cobblestone walkways wind past Ann Taylor, BCBG, Banana Republic, Godiva, Kenneth Cole, Jimmy Choo and Movado. All shopped-out? Take a leisurely gondola ride (p9).
☎ 414-4500 💻 www .venetian.com ✉ Venetian, 3355 Las Vegas Blvd S 🕙 10am-11pm Sun-Thu, to midnight Fri & Sat

Mandalay Place (2, C6)
M-Bay's new upscale commercial promenade houses 40 unique, fashion-forward boutiques, including Samantha Chang, Fornarina, Oilily, Sauvage, GF Ferre, Davidoff, Mulholland, Musette and Shoe Obsession.
☎ 632-7777 ✉ skybridge btwn Mandalay Bay & Luxor 🕙 10am-midnight

MGM Grand Studio Walk & Star Lane Shops (2, C5)
What to give the wannabe starlet who has everything? This Hollywood-themed mall may hold the answer. Designer luggage, costume jewelry and LV logo items are in the mix. At CBS TV City you can watch and rate TV pilots.
☎ 891-3300 💻 www .mgmgrand.com ✉ MGM, 3799 Las Vegas Blvd S 🕙 10am-10pm Ⓜ MGM Grand

Mirage Street of Shops (2, C3)
Euro-style spending on fancy feminine duds is all the rage at Actique, d.fine, DKNY, La Perla and Moschino. Leave the dog at home; bring your sunglasses.
☎ 791-7111 💻 www .mirage.com ✉ Mirage, 3400 Las Vegas Blvd S 🕙 9am-midnight

Monte Carlo's Street of Dreams (2, C5)
Chic shops along this tree-lined cobblestone avenue include the Medici Cigar Club, El Portal (luggage), Bon Vivant (women's wear), Elton's (men's garb), Lunettes (designer eyewear), Bubbles (bath and beauty products) and Crown Jewels. The

HyperMarket convenience store meets all your gourmet snacking needs. ☎ 730-7777 🖥 www .montecarlo.com ✉ Monte Carlo, 3770 Las Vegas Blvd S 🕐 9am-midnight

Neonopolis (3, D3)
The crown jewel in the Downtown redevelopment effort is notable for its collection of vintage neon signs. Twenty retail shops surround open courtyards, the Crown cinema complex (p68), a new gambling museum (p43) and alfresco dining options. The Fremont Street Experience (p20) is nearby. ☎ 477-0470 🖥 www .neonopolis.com ✉ 450 Fremont St 🕐 11am-11pm 🚌 108, 301, 302

Paris' Le Boulevard
(2, C4) Bally's and Paris are connected via this chichi cobblestone replica of Rue de la Paix. The winding promenade features French restaurants (pp52–3), lounges and boutiques. Highlights include fashion-

forward Lunettes eyewear, La Vogue designer lingerie, Clio Blue jewelry and La Cave gourmet food and wine. ☎ 946-4111 🖥 www .parislv.com ✉ Paris, 3655 Las Vegas Blvd S 🕐 10am-11pm Ⓜ Bally's & Paris

Rio's Masquerade Village Shops (2, B4)
Stroll faux 200-year-old Tuscan-tiled streets past mid-range retailers like La Valize (luggage, handbags and accessories), Roland's (evening and bridal wear), Timepieces (high-end watches and accessories), Fortune Cookie (Asian-inspired gifts), Elegant Pretenders (the finest in faux jewelry) and HippyChic (tie-dyed clothing). ☎ 252-7777 🖥 www .playrio.com ✉ Rio, 3700 W Flamingo Rd 🕐 10am-11pm 🚌 202

Showcase Mall (2, C5)
This 190,000-sq-ft 'architain-ment' archetype is aimed at the young MTV crowd. M&M's World, Ethel M

Chocolates and United Artists Cinemas (p68) vie for dollars from the demographers' wet dream. The interactive GameWorks (p21) arcade is in the basement. ☎ 597-3122 ✉ 3785 Las Vegas Blvd S 🕐 10am-midnight Ⓜ MGM Grand

Treasure Island Shops (2, C3) TI's stable of fashion-conscious gift shops and boutiques includes Rolex, Gucci and Calvin Klein. Cirque du Soleil merchandise is also available. ☎ 894-7111 🖥 www .treasureisland.com ✉ TI, 3300 Las Vegas Blvd S 🕐 10am-11pm

Via Bellagio (2, C4)
Bellagio's swish indoor promenade is home to the who's who of fashion-plate designers: Armani, Chanel, Dior, Fred Leighton (p40), Gucci, Hermés, Prada, Tiffany and Yves Saint Laurent. ☎ 693-7111 🖥 www .bellagio.com ✉ Bellagio, 3600 Las Vegas Blvd S 🕐 10am-midnight

CLOTHING & JEWELRY

Attic (3, C5)
A $1 'lifetime pass' (applied toward your first purchase) is required to enter this vintage emporium, but it's worth it, even if you don't buy. The 1st floor is mostly furnishings and hippie-chic clubwear. Upstairs, the1960s and '70s are strengths, with a smaller pre-1960s selection and a coffee bar with Greek grub. ☎ 388-4088 🖥 www .atticvintage.com ✉ 1018

S Main St 🕐 10am-6pm Mon-Sat 🚌 108, 207

Buffalo Exchange (2,F4)
Trade in your nearly new garb for cash or credit at this fashionable second-hand chain that runs a bit closer to the mainstream. They've combed through the dingy thrift store stuff and culled only the best 1940s to '70s vintage, clubwear, costuming goodies and

A girl's best friend.

contemporary dapper designer duds.
☎ 791-3960 ⊠ 4110 S Maryland Parkway
🕙 11am-8pm Mon-Sat, noon-7pm Sun 🚌 109, 202

Fred Leighton: Rare Collectible Jewels (2, C4)
Many Academy Awards–night adornments are on loan from the world's most-prestigious collection of antique jewelry. And in Las Vegas, unlike at the uptight NYC outlet, they'll let anyone try on finery that once belonged to royalty.
☎ 693-7050 ⊠ Via Bellagio, 3600 Las Vegas Blvd S 🕙 10am-midnight

Jewelers (2, E2)
Nevada's largest discount jewelry-chain stocks a wide selection of rings and necklaces. The Hilton branch is open around-the-clock to accommodate that 3am urge for a solid gold chain. Also at the Flamingo (p23).
☎ 893-9979 ⊠ Hilton, 3000 Paradise Rd
🕙 24/7/365 Ⓜ Hilton

Shopping on Via Bellagio

Retro Vintage Clothing (3, E4) Lots of timeless glam duds get cast off in this ahistorical town. Many end up at this upscale resale boutique, which specializes in men's and women's clothing from the 1920s through to the 1980s. Rentals available.
☎ 877-8989 ⊠ 1055 E Flamingo Rd 🕙 noon-6pm Tue-Sat 🚌 104, 206

Valentino's Zootsuit Connection (3, C5)
A sweet (and stylish!) husband-and-wife team outfit party-goers with upscale vintage apparel: fringed Western wear; felt hats and custom dresses.

Rentals and custom swinging zootsuits are a specialty.
☎ 383-9555 ⊠ 906 S 6th St 🕙 11am-5pm Mon-Sat 🚌 109, 206, 301, 302

Williams Costume Company (3, C5)
Williams has supplied The Strip's starlets with DIY costuming goods since 1957. Check out the headshots in the dressing rooms, then pick up some rhinestones, sequins, feathers, etc – you go girl. Friendly staff; costume rentals available.
☎ 384-1384 ⊠ 1226 S 3rd St 🕙 9am-5pm Mon-Fri 🚌 108, 206, 301, 302

CLOTHING & SHOE SIZES

Women's Clothing

Aust/UK	8	10	12	14	16	18
Europe	36	38	40	42	44	46
Japan	5	7	9	11	13	15
USA	6	8	10	12	14	16

Women's Shoes

Aust/USA	5	6	7	8	9	10
Europe	35	36	37	38	39	40
France only	35	36	38	39	40	42
Japan	22	23	24	25	26	27
UK	3½	4½	5½	6½	7½	8½

Men's Clothing

Aust	92	96	100	104	108	112
Europe	46	48	50	52	54	56

Japan	S	M	M		L	
UK/USA	35	36	37	38	39	40

Men's Shirts (Collar Sizes)

Aust/Japan	38	39	40	41	42	43
Europe	38	39	40	41	42	43
UK/USA	15	15½	16	16½	17	17½

Men's Shoes

Aust/UK	7	8	9	10	11	12
Europe	41	42	43	44½	46	47
Japan	26	27	27.5	28	29	30
USA	7½	8½	9½	10½	11½	12½

Measurements approximate only; try before you buy.

MUSIC & BOOKS

Gamblers Book Shop (3, D5) Longtime owner Edna Luckman (no joke) stocks thousands of out of print gambling-related titles. The friendly staff happily dispense valuable edge-beating advice. ☎ 382-7555, 800-522-1777 🖳 www.gamblersbook.com ✉ 630 S 11th St ⏰ 9am-5pm Mon-Sat 🚌 109, 206

Interstate Records (2, A4) Learn the fine art of turntablism at this cutting-edge mixology school and huge independent vinyl, video, CD and DVD outlet. ☎ 251-7551 ✉ 4780 Harmon Ave ⏰ 3pm-midnight Tue-Fri, noon-midnight Sat, noon-9pm Sun 🚌 104

Odyssey Records (3, C6) A large Latino selection sets this store apart from its chain counterparts. The rest of the discs are mostly mainstream rock and hip-hop, but there's a rack of listening stations and some

Literary Las Vegas – An Oxymoron?

The landmark anthology *Literary Las Vegas* (1995), edited by Mike Tronnes, excerpts some two dozen pieces spanning 40 years. Gonzo journalist Hunter S Thompson humorously recounts his trip to cover the Mint 400 Off-Road race in *Fear and Loathing in Las Vegas*. Mario Puzo's *Inside Las Vegas* provides an insightful look at what makes Sin City tick, from the inveterate gambler's perspective. Tom Wolfe's essays in *Kandy-Kolored Tangerine-Flaked Streamlined Baby* probe the swinging '60s Vegas.

jazz and world beat. ☎ 384-4040 ✉ 1600 Las Vegas Blvd S ⏰ 24/7 🚌 301, 302

Reading Room (2, C6) Vegas' newest indie bookshop is also its best. Highlights include a thoughtful selection of art and local-interest titles, plus some collectible editions. ☎ 632-9374 ✉ Mandalay Place, 3930 S Las Vegas Blvd ⏰ 10am-midnight 🚇 from Luxor

Record City (2, D1) Old skool DJs love this local chain because it's got the best selection of used vinyl in town. There are locations

a couple of blocks east of The Strip, plus three more stores around town. ☎ 369-6446 ✉ 300 & 553 E Sahara Ave ⏰ 10am-6pm Mon-Sat, noon-5pm Sun 🚌 108, 204

Virgin Megastore (2, C4) The undisputed mainstream music champ has a gaggle of listening stations, plus a digital kiosk near the cashier where you can listen to anything in the store. Upstairs, the magazine racks are the most impressive print media section. ☎ 696-7100 ✉ Forum Shops, 3500 Las Vegas Blvd S ⏰ 10am-midnight Ⓜ Flamingo & Caesars

Virgin Megastore

SPECIALIST SHOPS

Relics of past times

Apple Store (2, C3)
It's the hub for your non-PC digital lifestyle. Attend free hands-on demonstrations of all things 'i.' Query the savvy salespeople behind the Genius Bar about perplexing tech issues. Be wowed by the latest computer innovations in the theater.
☎ 650-9550 ✉ Fashion Show Mall, 3200 Las Vegas Blvd S ☽ 10am-9pm Mon-Fri, 10am-8pm Sat, 11am-6pm Sun

Downtown Arts & Antiques District (3, C5)
A significant antiques district has taken shape just south of Downtown in a series of funky stores inside older homes. Places worth checking out include the **Funk House** (3, C5; ☎ 678-6278; 1228 S Casino Center Blvd), **Gypsy Caravan** (3, C5; ☎ 868-3302; 1302 S 3rd St) and **Yana's Junk** (3, C5; ☎ 388-0051; 201 E Colorado Ave). ✉ Colorado Ave btwn Main & 3rd Sts ☽ varies ☒ 108, 301, 302

Houdini's Magic Shop (2, C3)
The legendary escape artist's legacy lives on at this shop packed with gags, pranks and magic tricks. Magicians perform and each purchase includes a free private lesson. Also at Bally's (p22) and Desert Passage (pp37–8).
☎ 796-0301 ✉ Venetian, 3355 Las Vegas Blvd S ☽ 10am-11pm Sun-Thu, to midnight Fri & Sat

Guggenheim Store (2, C3)
The Venetian's museum (p9) gift shop stocks items that are as classy as the art collection. A discerning spot to find an aesthetically pleasing souvenir.
☎ 414-2400 ✉ Venetian, 3355 Las Vegas Blvd S ☽ 9am-9pm

Metropolitan Museum of Art Store (2, C4)
NYC's Met is known for its reproductions and singular gift items. Sales of books, scarves, stationery, prints and jewelry support the museum's educational mission.
☎ 691-2506 ✉ Desert Passage, 3663 Las Vegas Blvd S ☽ 10am-10pm Sun-Thu, to midnight Fri & Sat

Niketown (2, C4)
The speccy kicks might not help you jump higher, but they'll certainly send your account balance southward. For sports fans, the memorabilia and video screens are worth a look.
☎ 650-8888 ✉ Forum Shops, 3500 Las Vegas Blvd S ☽ 10am-11pm Sun-Thu, to midnight Fri & Sat Ⓜ Flamingo & Caesars

Wine Cellar (2, B4)
Rio's classy subterranean tasting room stocks 45,000 bottles from 3000 vintners, all assembled by an ex-president of the International Court of Master Sommeliers. Single malt Scotch tasting–flights and exotic chocolates round out the amazing, must-taste collection.
☎ 777-7614 ✉ Rio, 3700 W Flamingo Rd ☽ 3pm-midnight Mon-Fri, noon-midnight Sat & Sun ☒ 202

Guggenheim Museum Store

GAMBLING GOODS

If you fancy shoving coins into a slot machine, consider buying one. There are many places selling new and reconditioned slots and video poker machines. Visit the Gamblers Book Shop (p41) for tips on beating the almighty house edge.

Gamblers General Store (3, C4) Nevada's largest inventory of slot machines includes a full house of the very latest digital models and vintage machines. The gaming tables are identical to those found in many casinos. There is a great book, gift and souvenir selection, too.
☎ 382-9903, 800-322-2447 🖳 www.gamblers generalstore.com ✉ 800 S Main St 🕒 9am-5pm 🚌 108, 207

Lost Vegas Gambling Museum & Store (3, D3) Downtown at Neonopolis, this museum sheds light on Sin City's checkered past and sells slices of history, from antique slot machines to portable souvenirs like vintage poker chips, match-books and photographs.
☎ 385-1883 🖳 www .neonopolis.com ✉ Neonopolis, 450 Fremont St 💲 museum $2.50/1.25 🕒 10am-9pm 🚌 301, 302

Showcase Slots & Antiquities (2, B4) Save quarters in your own stylish piggy bank: buy a vintage or modern one-armed bandit or video poker machine. Or a nostalgic game-room antique like a Wurlitzer jukebox or retro candy machine.
☎ 740-5722, 888-522-7568 ✉ 4305 S Industrial Rd 🖳 www.showcases lots.com 🕒 9am-5pm Mon-Sat, 10am-3pm Sun 🚌 105

NAUGHTY NOVELTIES

In a town with as many strip clubs as gas stations, it should come as little surprise that the adult apparel business is ba-bah-booming. All those hard-working beefy guys and sultry women obviously don't have time to make their own G-strings and tasseled undies. There's also a full-service lingerie shop inside Olympic Garden (p67).

Adult Superstore (2, B5) Popular with couples, this enormous, well-lit porn warehouse has more pussies than the SPCA: toys, books, magazines, videos, tasteful 'marital enhancement products' and titillating accessories. Single guys gravitate toward the XXX arcade upstairs.
☎ 798-0144 ✉ 3850 W Tropicana Ave 🕒 24/7/365 🚌 201

Bare Essentials (2, A1) Pros swear by BE for business attire. It's heavy on theme wear – lots of cheerleader and schoolgirl outfits. There is a good selection of knee-high boots and many of the men's and women's fantasy fashions come in plus sizes.
☎ 247-4711 ✉ 4029 W Sahara Ave 🕒 10am-7pm Mon-Sat, noon-6pm Sun 🚌 201

A Slightly Sinful Adventure (3, C5) Many of the outfits here are layered: tiny outer garments followed by much tinier undergarments. For voyeurs, admiring the goods in the presence of the professional clientele can make a visit worth the effort.
☎ 387-1006 ✉ 1232 Las Vegas Blvd S 🕒 10am-10pm Sun-Thu, to midnight Fri & Sat 🚌 301, 302

WEIRD & WONDERFUL

Bonanza Gifts Shop (2, D1)
If it's not the 'World's Largest Gift Shop,' it's damn near close. The amazing kitsch selection of only-in-Vegas souvenirs includes entire aisles of dice clocks, snow globes, sassy slogan T-shirts, shot glasses and XXX gags.
☎ 385-7359 ✉ 2460 Las Vegas Blvd S ⏰ 11am-midnight 🚌 301, 302

Gun Store (1, B4)
Attention wannabe Schwarzeneggers: this high-powered shop offers gun rentals, live submachine-gun rounds in its indoor video training range, and security, safety and con-cealed arms permit classes. Not to mention the massive cache of weapons for sale.
☎ 454-1110 🖥 www.thegunstorelasvegas.com ✉ 2900 E Tropicana Ave ⏰ 9am-6:30pm 🚌 205

Imperial Palace Auto Collection (2, C4)
Everything on display is for sale on consignment (sorry, no test drives) at the indoor antique and collectibles lot on the 5th floor of the parking garage. See p27 for a full review.
☎ 794-3174 🖥 www.autocollections.com ✉ Imperial Palace, 3535 Las Vegas Blvd S ⏰ 9:30am-9:30pm

Paradise Electro Stimulations (3, B6)
The 'Tiffany's of Fetish Boutiques' is tucked discreetly away on the wrong side of the tracks. It's the exotic, erotic and invigorating home of owner Dante Amore's legendary Auto-Erotic Chair, which must be seen (and felt) to be believed. Yeow-ch.
☎ 474-2991, 800-339-6953 🖥 www.peselectro

Float away in the art district

.com ✉ 1509 W Oakey Blvd ⏰ 10am-7pm Mon-Fri, noon-5pm Sat 🚌 205

Rainbow Feather Dyeing Company (3, C5)
Where to satisfy that boa fetish? Need turkey, chicken, duck, goose, pheasant, ostrich or peacock quills? Rainbow stocks a positively fabulous selection of fine feathers in every possible shade.
☎ 598-0998 🖥 www.rainbowfeatherco.com ✉ 1036 S Main St ⏰ 9am-5pm Mon-Fri 🚌 108

Eating

Sin City is an unmatched eating adventure. Since Wolfgang Puck brought Spago to Caesars in 1992, celebrity Iron Chefs have taken up residence in nearly every megaresort. With so many star-struck tables to choose from, stakes are high and there are many overhyped eating gambles.

Cheap buffets and loss-leader meal deals still exist, mostly Downtown, but the gourmet quotient is high. It's slim pickings for vegetarians, with only a few options at most places – buffet salad bars are your best bet. For the most-authentic ethnic flavors, look to the Eastside or Westside.

> ## Meal Costs
> The pricing symbols used in this chapter indicate the cost of a main dinner course, excluding tax, tips or drinks.
>
> | | |
> |---|---|
> | $ | under $10 |
> | $$ | $10-19 |
> | $$$ | $20-29 |
> | $$$$ | over $30 |

Drinks
Every sit-down eatery serves alcohol (the drinking age is 21; ID checks are de rigueur). Most upscale places pour wine by the glass and several five-star restaurants have world-class wine lists and sommeliers. Request bottled water, since the taste of tap water here can ruin a good meal.

Tipping & Tax
The standard gratuity is 15% to 20% before tax; that's double the 7.5% meal tax, plus an added toke for exceptional service. A service charge of 15% to 18% is often added for groups of six or more. At buffets, it's standard to leave a tip of at least $1 per person.

Reservations & Dress Code
Book as far in advance as possible for fancier restaurants. Reservations at the biggest names are essential on weekends – ask your concierge for assistance. Many places offer online booking. Unless otherwise noted, the dress code at upscale eateries is business casual. At the most-famous places, jackets are required for men – inquire when booking.

Meal Times
Las Vegans are on the go 24/7, so it's always possible to get a meal – but hardly ever a vegan one. Every major casino has a 24-hour café, and breakfast is often served nonstop. Weekend champagne brunch buffets (9am to 4:30pm) are a hot ticket. Lunch begins around 11am and runs until 3pm. Dinner starts promptly at 5pm (so you can catch an early show) and ends around 10pm weekdays or 11pm on weekends.

THE STRIP

Aladdin (2, C4)

Dining options include Commander's Palace ($$$$) for Sunday jazz brunch and authentic Creole cuisine; Crustacean ($$$$) for French-Vietnamese seafood; Elements ($$$$) for surf-and-turf fare; St James at the London Club ($$$$) for top-notch global cuisine; Tremezzo ($$$) for Northern Italian; Bonsai Sushi Bar ($$$); the superb Spice Market Buffet ($$); and the 24-hour Zanzibar Cafe ($).

Todai Seafood & Sushi Buffet (2, C4) $$$

Japanese Seafood
Inside Desert Passage (pp37–8), this all-you-can-gorge 160ft spread features 15 salads and 40 types of sushi. Lobster, shellfish and crab legs are added to the mix at dinnertime.
☎ 892-0021 ✉ Aladdin, 3663 Las Vegas Blvd S (entrance on Harmon Ave) ☷ 11:30am-2:30pm & 5:30-9:30pm, to 10pm Fri-Sun ☷ under 12 half-price

Bally's (2, C4)

Bally's eateries are all solid but none go out on a limb. Other reliable options include Bally's Steakhouse ($$$$); the Big Kitchen Buffet ($$); and the 24-hour Sidewalk Café ($).

Bally's Steakhouse (2, C4) $$$$

Gourmet Brunch
Indulge in the best – and most-expensive – Sunday brunch in town. Ice sculptures and lavish flower

Gourmet Rooms with a View

When the panorama is important and price is not, ascend to Alizé (p57), Binion's Ranch Steak House (p55), Eiffel Tower Restaurant (p52), Top of the World (p53) or the VooDoo Café & Lounge (p57). For romantic fountain views, try Mon Ami Gabi (p53) or any of the Bellagio's (pp47–8) or Wynn Las Vegas' (p72) lakefront restaurants.

arrangements abound at the Sterling Brunch, as do food stations featuring roast duckling, steak Diane, seared salmon with beet butter sauce – you get the idea. Reservations suggested.
☎ 967-7999 ✉ Bally's Steakhouse, 3645 Las Vegas Blvd S ☷ 5:30-10.30pm Mon-Sat, 9:30am-2:30pm Sun

Barbary Coast (2, C4)

Michael's (2, C4) $$$$

Continental
Lavished with the Barbary Coast's signature Tiffany-style stained glass, this top-drawer gourmet room does four dinner seatings daily. Prime à la carte delicacies include chateaubriand and live Maine lobster. It's old

Vegas at its most rococo. Reservations essential; coats required.
☎ 737-7111 ✉ Downstairs, Barbary Coast, 3595 Las Vegas Blvd S ☷ seatings 6pm, 6:30pm, 9pm & 9:30pm

Victorian Room (2, C4) $

American
This lively, central, 24-hour coffee shop sports deep red-leather booths, stained glass and polished brass. Graveyard specialties like New York steak-and-eggs ($5.95) and 24/7 T-bone or prime rib deals that don't cut corners make it a favorite after-hours hangout.
☎ 737-7111 ✉ Casino level, Barbary Coast, 3595 Las Vegas Blvd S ☷ 24/7/365 ☷

Bellagio (2, C4)

Bellagio's culinary stable, featuring seven James Beard award-winners, runs the gamut from haute cuisine to Vegas' best 24/7 casual comfort food. For impeccably fresh seafood, don't miss Michael Mina ($$$$), the new incarnation of Aqua.

Buffet at Bellagio (2, C4) $$$
Buffet
The Bellagio rightfully takes top honors for Vegas' best live-action buffet. The sumptuous all-you-can-eat spread includes such crowd-pleasers as smoked salmon, roast turkey, and innumerable creative Chinese, Japanese and Italian dishes. ☎ 693-7111 ✉ Casino level, Bellagio, 3600 Las Vegas Blvd S ⏱ 8am-11pm Mon-Fri ♿

Café Bellagio (2, C4) $$
Café
Bellagio's all-hours eatery is among the best in town. The menu features exciting twists on traditional American favorites. Big draws are the delicious coffees, flowery setting and its gorgeous views of the swimming pool and garden areas. ☎ 693-7111 ✉ Conservatory, Bellagio, 3600 Las Vegas Blvd S ⏱ 24/7/365 ♿

Circo (2, C4) $$$
Northern Italian
Feast on northern Italian delights at this whimsical big top–inspired venue. The restaurant overlooks the dancing fountains on faux Lake Como. Rustic, yet complex, Tuscan entrees, such as pan-seared foie gras with mission fig compote, perform well with an international cellar of 500 wines. Jackets and ties are required. ☎ 693-7223 ✉ Casino level, Bellagio, 3600 Las Vegas Blvd S ⏱ 11:30am-2:30pm, 5:30-10:30pm Mon-Fri, brunch 11:30am-2:30pm Sat & Sun

Best Rabelaisian Feasts

When it comes to groaning boards, the old adage 'You get what you pay for' was never more true. Most buffets feature live-action stations specializing in sushi, seafood, pasta, stir-fries and so on. Among the standard entrees at the upscale resorts: shrimp, lobster claws, antipasti, beef tenderloin, carved-to-order roast meats, fresh fruit, various soups and lots of salad material. Buffet prices, like hotel rates, fluctuate. Generally, expect to pay $7 to $15 for breakfast, from $15 to $50 for brunch, $10 to $20 for lunch and from $15 for dinner.

A new wave of unlimited gourmet eating has hit Vegas. Bellagio (above), Luxor (p18) and Paris (pp52–3) compete for top honors in the class-act category, with the Mirage (p51) running a close second. Off The Strip Rio's (p57) buffets are the best. Bally's Steakhouse (opposite) lays on the best Sunday champagne spread, while the House of Blues (p50) Sunday gospel brunch is the most unique.

Join the queue at the Venetian

Jasmine (2, C4) $$$$
Hong Kong Chinese
An elegant lakefront eatery surrounded by lovely gardens. Executive chef Philip Lo offers modern takes on Cantonese, Sichuan and Hunan classics like braised superior shark fin with silver sprouts and Jin Wah ham.
☎ 693-8166 ✉ Casino level, Bellagio, 3600 Las Vegas Blvd S ⏲ 5:30-10pm

Le Cirque (2, C4) $$$$
Modern French
Top toque Marc Poidevin pairs artful haute cuisine with world-class wines in a joyous, intimate setting. Rabbit fricassee with Riesling, chanterelles and fava beans is a signature dish. Three-ring tasting menu $85, five acts $115. Jacket and tie required.
☎ 693-7223 ✉ Casino level, Bellagio, 3600 Las Vegas Blvd S ⏲ 5:30-10pm

Noodles (2, C4) $$
Pan-Asian Noodle Bar
This late-night noodle joint doles out bowls from across the Orient. The decor is stylish modern. Dim sum and Hong Kong-style BBQ make guest appearances.
☎ 693-7111 ✉ Casino level, Bellagio, 3600 Las Vegas Blvd S ⏲ 11am-2am, dim sum 11am-3pm Fri-Sun 🐟

Olives (2, C4) $$$
Mediterranean
Todd English, a Bostonian native, dishes up a homage to the ancient life-giving fruit. Flatbread pizzas, housemade pasta and

flame-licked meats get top billing. Window seats face the bustling open kitchen while patio tables overlook Lake Como. Good wine list.
☎ 693-8181 ✉ Via Bellagio, Bellagio, 3600 Las Vegas Blvd S ⏲ 11am-2:30pm & 5-10:30pm

Picasso (2, C4) $$$$
French-Spanish
Five-star chef Julian Serrano delivers artistic Franco-Iberian fusion in a museum-like setting. Original eponymous masterpieces complement entrees like the sautéed fallow deer medallions and seafood boudin. Vaulted ceilings and wooden beams create an unpretentious Mediterranean feel. Linger on the patio over a digestif. Prix fixe ($85) and degustation ($95) menus are recommended. Jacket and tie suggested. Reservations essential and difficult.
☎ 693-7223 ✉ Casino level, Bellagio, 3600 Las Vegas Blvd S ⏲ 6-9:30pm Wed-Mon

Prime Steakhouse (2, C4) $$$$
Steakhouse-Seafood
Pay a visit to this luxurious contemporary chophouse with plenty of stylistic nods to 1930s speakeasies. Trademark dishes include scallops with caper-raisin emulsion and caramelized cauliflower, and live Maine lobster with braised artichokes. Elegant bar, superb service, robust wine list. Jackets preferred.
☎ 693-7223 ✉ Via Bellagio, Bellagio, 3600 Las Vegas Blvd S ⏲ 5:30-10pm

Shintaro (2, C4) $$$$
Japanese
There's a bit of everything here: premium sake, sublime sushi, *teppanyaki* (tabletop BBQ grills) and tea ceremony-style *kaiseki* (artfully presented Japanese tapas) tasting menus ($45 to $95). Don't miss the kaleidoscopic jellyfish aquarium behind the sushi bar.
☎ 693-7223 ✉ Via Bellagio, Bellagio, 3600 Las Vegas Blvd S ⏲ 5:30-10pm

Caesars Palace & Forum Shops (2, C4)
Options include Bobby Flay's new Mesa Grill ($$$); Bradley Ogden ($$$$) for gourmet farm-fresh fare; Empress Court ($$) for Chinese; Neros ($$$) for steaks and seafood; and the decadent Palatium Buffet ($$).

808 (2, C4) $$$
Pacific Rim-Seafood
Chef Jean-Marie Josselin dials Hawaii ('eight-oh-eight') daily on the coconut wireless to procure the raw goods that fuel this tropical island-themed delight. The result is a creative mingling of French, Mediterranean, Indian and Pacific Rim elements. Many locals regard this as their city's top seafood stop.
☎ 877-346-4642 ✉ Casino level, Caesars Palace, 3570 Las Vegas Blvd S ⏲ 5:30-10:30pm, to 11pm Fri & Sat

Chinois (2, C4) $$$
Chinese-French
Forget designer pizza. Peripatetic chef Wolfgang

Puck scores again with his signature Eurasian fusion served in a soothing, artistic Far Eastern atmosphere. Try the Shanghai lobster with a premium cold sake. Trendy dance club upstairs.
☎ 737-9700 ✉ Forum Shops, Caesars Palace, 3570 Las Vegas Blvd S ✦ 10:30am-10:30pm Ⓥ

Hyakumi (2, C4) $$$$
Japanese
One of Vegas' top Japanese joints, 'yah-*coo*-me' (literally '100 tastes') offers diners a choice of *teppan-yaki* grill table or sushi bar seating. Gracious waitstaff don traditional obi and kimonos, and the decor is rustic country village, with a garden atmosphere.
☎ 877-346-4642 ✉ Casino level, Caesars Palace, 3570 Las Vegas Blvd S ✦ 5:30-10:30pm, to 11pm Fri & Sat

Palm (2, C4) $$$$
Steakhouse-Seafood
Vegas' premier surf-and-turf haven is lauded for its jumbo Nova Scotia lobster and gigantic portions – but prepare to be clawed by the prices. The $16 prix fixe lunch, however, is one of the best deals in town. The shrimp cocktails and prime steaks are fantastic.
☎ 732-7256 ✉ Forum Shops, Caesars Palace, 3570 S Las Vegas Blvd ✦ 11:30am-11pm

Stage Deli (2, C4) $
Deli
Sky-high sandwiches, named after gourmand celebs like Wilt Chamberlin (corned beef with sauerkraut

World-Class Wine Lists

Andrés (p55), Aureole (p50), Delmonico Steakhouse (p53), Emeril's (p51), Picasso (opposite) and Pinot Brasserie (p54) all have first-rate wine lists, stellar sommeliers and impressive, expense account stretching selections.

Sugar and spice and all things nice at Aureole

and Swiss), and a huge selection of heaping sides, add up to one thing: indigestion. Also dishes up bagels and lox for breakfast at the MGM Grand Studio Walk (p38).
☎ 893-4045 ✉ Forum Shops, Caesars Palace, 3570 Las Vegas Blvd S ✦ 11am-11pm, to midnight Fri & Sat ♿

Terrazza (2, C4) $$$$
Northern Italian
Rustic, well-prepared Tuscan fare, like wood-fired pizzas from the dining room oven, are served in a delicious poolside setting. The glass-enclosed pavilion seating features Garden of the Gods views. The plush lounge has live jazz Wednesday to Sunday.
☎ 731-7568 ✉ Pool

level near Roman & Palace Towers, Caesars Palace, 3570 Las Vegas Blvd S ✦ 5:30-11pm Tue-Sat

Circus Circus (2, D2)

Steak House (2, D2) $$$$
Steakhouse
In a town filled with meat mongers, the one under the big top is top-drawer. All clowning aside, this place takes itself very seriously, resembling a British hunting lodge with lots of dark wood and an elegant bar. Good Sunday champagne brunch.
☎ 794-3767 ✉ Circus Circus, 2880 Las Vegas Blvd S ✦ 5-11pm Tue-Sun, to midnight Sat, brunch seatings 9:30am, 11:30am & 1:30pm Sun ♿

Mandalay Bay & Four Seasons (2, C6)

M-bay's outstanding dining options include 3950 ($$$$) for steaks and seafood; the high-quality Bayside Buffet ($$); the Noodle Shop ($) for late-night Chinese and the 24-hour Raffles Cafe ($$). Hubert Keller is scheduled to open a branch of the famed Fleur de Lys in early 2005.
Reservations ☎ 632-5300

Aureole (2,C6) $$$$
New American
Chef Charlie Palmer's inspired seasonal American dishes like spice-crusted tuna with foie gras soar to new heights here. The prix fixe tasting menus ($95) are pure art and it's worth ordering wine just to watch the stewards ascend the four-story tower. Extensive wine list, formal dress. Reservations essential and difficult.
☎ 632-7401 🖳 www .aureolelv.com
✉ Near west valet, Mandalay Bay, 3960 Las Vegas Blvd S 🕑 6-10:30pm

Border Grill (2,C6) $$
Mexican
Overlooking Mandalay Beach, this modern stylish restaurant features fare as seen on the Food Network's *Too Hot Tamales*. The tortilla soup, green corn tamales and sautéed rock shrimp pass for authentic Nayarit fare.
☎ 632-7403
✉ Near Shark Reef, Mandalay Bay, 3960 Las Vegas Blvd S
🕑 11:30am-11pm 🚻

Big Bucks Burger
Since when is a hamburger worth $60? When it's built with Kobe beef, sautéed foie gras, shaved truffles and Madeira sauce. Chef Hubert Keller (of San Francisco's famed Fleur de Lys) serves up his signature Rossini burger, burger-themed desserts and other gourmet comfort treats daily at the **Burger Bar** (2, C6; ☎ 632-9364; 🕑 10:30am-11pm Thu-Sun, to 1am Fri & Sat) in Mandalay Palace, the shopping mall linking Luxor and Mandalay Bay.

Charlie Palmer Steak (2,C6) $$$$
Steakhouse
Artisan-aged beef is grilled to perfection at this classy hideaway. Impressive wine list; business casual dress. Reservations essential.
☎ 632-5120 ✉ Four Seasons , Mandalay Bay, 3960 Las Vegas Blvd S
🕑 5-10:15pm, bar 3pm-midnight

China Grill (2,C6) $$$$
Chinese
Ambitious, oversized Marco Polo–inspired takes on traditional pan-Asian signature dishes like Kobe beef carpaccio infused with Thai chili oil. After dinner on Wednesday, the opulent sunken lounge transforms into the hip Dragon club. Don't miss the granite dance floor and outhouse-style unisex bathrooms.
☎ 632-7404 ✉ Near west valet, Mandalay Bay, 3960 Las Vegas Blvd S
🕑 5:30pm-midnight

House of Blues (2,C6) $$
American-Southern
This homey roadhouse (burgers, salads, BBQ) is a good pit stop before a show (pp65–6) and a pre-show dinner receipt whisks you past the show door line. The swampy bayou atmosphere is enhanced by eccentric outsider folk art. Skip church: the uplifting Sunday Gospel Brunch includes unlimited champagne.
☎ 632-7600 ✉ Casino level, Mandalay Bay, 3960 Las Vegas Blvd S 🕑 8am-midnight, to 1am Fri & Sat; brunch 10am & 1pm Sun 🚻

Red Square (2,C6) $$$
Postmodern Russian
How post-perestroika: a headless Lenin invites you to join your comrades for a tipple behind the red curtain. There's a solid ice bar, heaps of caviar, a huge selection of frozen vodkas and infusions – and loaner sable fur coats for when you step into the locker!
☎ 632-7407 ✉ Near west valet, Mandalay Bay, 3960 Las Vegas Blvd S
🕑 5:30-10:30pm

rumjungle (2,C6) $$$
Brazilian-Steakhouse
It's like a culinary episode of *Survivor*, featuring all-you-can-eat *rodizio* skewers of all manner of meats. A tower of 150 firewaters looms over the open fire pit and dueling giant conga

drums After hours, it turns into a dance club.

☎ 632-7408 ✉ Near west valet, Mandalay Bay, 3960 Las Vegas Blvd S ⏱ 5:30-10:30pm

Trattoria del Lupo (2,C6) $$$
Italian
Wolfgang's puckish Del Lupo features casual rustic decor, an exhibition kitchen, a good bar at the center of the dining room and a decent wine selection. Housemade charcuterie and heavenly desserts.

☎ 740-5522 ✉ Near west valet, Mandalay Bay, 3960 Las Vegas Blvd S ⏱ 11:30am-11pm, to midnight Fri & Sat

Verandah Cafe (2,C6) $$$
Eclectic American
This comfortable yet elegant oasis is about as far away from the ding-ding-ding as you can get. Weekend brunch buffet, Night Owl service and afternoon English tea are worth the trip from anywhere on The Strip. Casual dress; poolside patio seating.

☎ 632-5000 ✉ Four Seasons, Mandalay Bay, 3960 Las Vegas Blvd S ⏱ 6am-10pm ♿

MGM Grand (2, C5)
Good options include the Grand Buffet ($$); Craft-steak ($$$) for tavern fare; pan-Asian Grand Wok ($$) for sushi; Diego ($$) for tequila drinks and modern Mexican; the sleek Fiamma Trattoria ($$$); Pearl ($$$) for Chinese; Shibuya ($$$) for sublime sushi; Seablue

($$$$) for the catch of the minute; Wolfgang Puck's Bar & Grill ($$) for California flair and the 24-hour Studio Cafe ($$).

Reservations ☎ 877-793-7111, 🖥 www.mgm grand.com

Emeril's (2,C5) $$$
Seafood-Cajun/Creole
The Crescent City's most televised chef, Emeril Lagasse, cranks it up a notch at his New Orleans fish house, with barbecued oysters and lobster cheesecake. The wine list is a *Wine Spectator* award-winner, and the banana cream pie drizzled with caramel is sumptin' else.

☎ 891-7374 ✉ Studio Walk, MGM Grand, 3799 Las Vegas Blvd S ⏱ 11am-2:30pm & 5:30-10:30pm

Nobhill (2,C5) $$$$
Seafood-Californian
Michael Mina, a James Beard award–winning chef (p47) brings the best of Northern California's gourmet cornucopia, including housemade sourdough breads, farmstead cheeses and Monterey Bay abalone. True to NoCal form, the ambience is laid-back yet elegant. Five-course tasting menus and bar seating.

☎ 891-7337 ✉ Casino level, MGM Grand, 3799 Las Vegas Blvd S ⏱ 5:30-10:30pm

Mirage (2, C3)
Savory options include the Cravings Buffet ($$); California Pizza Kitchen ($$); Kokomo's steakhouse ($$$); Mikado ($$$) for Japanese; Moongate ($$$)

for Chinese; Onda ($$$) for Italian; and the 24-hour Caribe Café ($).

Reservations ☎ 866-339-4566, 🖥 www.mirage.com

Renoir (2, C3) $$$$
French
A frequent award winner for the best food in town, chef Alessandro Stratta's romantic masterpiece is decorated with originals by the namesake painter. The seasonal cuisine (think roasted sea bass with coconut salad) is as haute and imaginative as the service is suave. Jackets and reservations suggested; no smoking. World-class wine list. Prix fixe menu $90.

☎ 791-7353 ✉ Casino level, Mirage, 3400 Las Vegas Blvd S ⏱ 5:30-9:30pm Tue-Sat

Samba Brazilian Steakhouse (2, C3) $$$
Brazilian-Steakhouse
The spit-roasted meats, poultry and seafood keep on coming at this tropical-themed *rodizio* buffet. À la carte options and wild cocktails are also on offer.

☎ 791-7111 ✉ Casino level, Mirage, 3400 Las Vegas Blvd S ⏱ 5-10:30pm

Monte Carlo (2, C5)
Options include Andre's (p55) for French; Blackstone's Steakhouse ($$$); the above-average Buffet ($$); the Monte Carlo Pub & Brewery (p59); Market City Caffe ($); a fast-food court ($); and a 24-hour café ($). The HyperMarket convenience store also has snacks.

Big Deal Dinners
When it's time to seal a big deal, book a table at Aureole (p50), Charlie Palmer Steak (p50), Delmonico Steakhouse (opposite), Michael Mina (p47), Nobu (p56) or Prime Steakhouse (p48).

Nibble at Nobu

Dragon Noodle Company (2,C5) $$
Chinese
This noodle spot is a reasonably authentic slurp of Hong Kong. Meals are displayed for diners' inspection, the food is grilled in plain sight and there's a tea bar. Try the air-dried roast duck (all the flavor, half the fat).
☎ 730-7965 ☐ www.dragonnoodleco.com ✉ Casino level, Monte Carlo, 3770 Las Vegas Blvd S ☺ 11am-11pm, to midnight Fri & Sat

New York-New York (2, C5)
Palatable options include Il Fornaio ($$$) for Italian; Nine Fine Irishmen ($$) for live music and upscale pub grub; Chin Chin ($) for Chinese; Nathan's Famous Hot Dogs ($); New York Pretzel stands ($); Schrafft's Ice Cream ($) and the Village Eateries ($) for fast-food noshes.

America (2,C5) $$
American
A fanciful bas-relief US map hangs over this reliable, patriotic all-hours eatery. Many go red-white-and-blue in the face trying to pick something from the extensive menu of all-American fare. Extensive bi-coastal beer and wine selection.
☎ 740-6451 ✉ Adjacent registration, New York-New York, 3790 Las Vegas Blvd S ☺ 24/7/365

Gallagher's (2, C5) $$$$
Steakhouse
You can't ignore the house specialty, dry aged sirloin, in the meat lockers out front. The rest of the USDA-choice menu's surf-and-turf offerings are justifiably famous. To whet your appetite, try the burgundy escargot.
☎ 740-6450 ✉ Greenwich Village, New York-New York, 3790 Las Vegas Blvd S ☺ 4-11pm

Gonzalez y Gonzalez (2, C5) $$
Mexican
There's *un poco de* Tex in this relatively authentic tequila cantina. You won't find *pozole* (Mexico's answer to matzo ball soup) and *pollo frito* (whole fried tilapia with avocado relish) on many menus in Houston. *Buen provecho.*
☎ 740-6455 ✉ Greenwich Village, New York-New York, 3790 Las Vegas Blvd S ☺ 11am-11pm, to midnight Sat & Sun, bar 11-1am, to 2am Fri & Sat

Paris (2, C4)
Good options run by a cordon bleu–trained culinary staff of 500 are the 24-hour Café Île St Louis ($$); pastries at JJ's Boulangerie ($); steaks at Les Artistes ($$$); Italian at Le Provençal ($$$); crepes on Rue de la Paix (p39); and Caribbean at Ortanique ($$$).

Eiffel Tower Restaurant (2, C4) $$$$
French
The adage about the better the view, the worse the food doesn't apply here. Views of The Strip and Bellagio's fountains are as breathtaking as the near-perfect renditions of haute classics like foie gras. Tasting menu recommended. Good wine list. Reservations required; dress business casual.
☎ 948-6937 ✉ 11th fl, Eiffel Tower, Paris, 3655 Las Vegas Blvd S ☺ 5:30-10pm

Le Village Buffet (2, C4) $$$
Regional French–Seafood
Selections from France's various regions are represented at distinct cooking stations, with an emphasis on seafood. Fresh fruit and cheeses, cracked crab legs

and a wide range of pastries make the Village arguably the best-value buffet on The Strip. The popular Sunday brunch includes unlimited champagne.

☎ 946-7000 ✉ Rue de la Paix, Paris, 3655 Las Vegas Blvd S 🕓 7:30am-10:30pm, brunch 11:30am-4:30pm Sun

Mon Ami Gabi (2, C4) $$$
French-Seafood
Think charming Champs Élysées bistro. This elevated patio seating (first come, first served) in the shadow of the Eiffel Tower is the only Stripside alfresco dining and affords great people-watching. There's a raw seafood bar and the steak frites are *parfait*. Good, reasonable wine list.

☎ 944-4224 ✉ Paris, 3655 Las Vegas Blvd S 🕓 11:30am-3:30pm & 5-11pm, to midnight Fri & Sat

Stratosphere (2, D1)
Top of the World (2, D1) $$$$
Continental
A dressy, revolving romantic roost perched atop the Stratosphere Tower (p22). While taking in the cloud-level views, patrons enjoy impeccable service and delicious (if overpriced) mains such as veal, lobster and almond-crusted salmon.

Reservations recommended. Good wine list.

☎ 380-7711, 800-998-6937 🖥 www.strato spherehotel.com ✉ 2000 Las Vegas Blvd S 🕓 10am-3pm & 6-11pm, to midnight Fri & Sat

Tropicana (2, C5)
Worthwhile options include the Savanna Steakhouse ($$$) and Pietro's ($$$$) gourmet room. Avoid the buffet.

Mizuno's (2, C5) $$$
Japanese-Steakhouse
Chefs prepare tempura, shrimp, lobster, chicken and steak tableside on teppan-yaki grills with swordsmen-like moves. The restaurant itself is a work of art, with gorgeous marble floors and many Japanese antiques. Reservations required.

☎ 739-2713 🖥 www .tropicanalv.com ✉ Ca-sino level, Tropicana, 3801 Las Vegas Blvd S 🕓 5:30-10:45pm

Venetian & Grand Canal Shoppes (2, C3)
This mid-Strip bite of Italy is appropriately a world-class dining destination with 17 restaurants. Reservations (☎ 414-4300; www .venetian.com) and formal dress are a must for the fancier places. Dining options include Canaletto

($$$) for Northern Italian; casual Canyon Ranch Café ($$$) for spa cuisine; sushi at Tsunami ($$) and Noodle Asia ($) for steaming late-night slurps.

Bouchon (2, C3) $$$$
French
Napa Valley wonder boy Thomas Keller's new rendition of a Lyonnaise bistro features an award-winning menu of seasonal classics. The poolside setting complements the oyster bar, extensive raw seafood selection, super wine list and decadent desserts.

☎ 414-6200 ✉ Venezia Tower, Venetian, 3355 Las Vegas Blvd S 🕓 5-10:30pm, oyster bar & cocktail lounge 3pm-midnight

Delmonico Steakhouse (2, C3) $$$$
Steakhouse
Bam: it's celeb chef Emeril Lagasse's greatest gourmet hits, as seen on TV. The cuts are ready for prime time, the influences are Creole and the chateaubriand-for-two is carved tableside. Big oak doors open into a vaulted ceiling space with a petite grand piano.

☎ 414-3737 ✉ Casino level, Venetian, 3355 Las Vegas Blvd S 🕓 11:30am-2pm & 5:30-10:30pm, to 11pm Fri & Sat

Grand Lux Café (2, C3) $$
Eclectic Café-Bistro
A sophisticated quick bite, if you don't want to stray too far from the tables. The plates of global comfort food are piled high, the ambience is elegant yet

---

After-Hours Eats
With over two hundred 24-hour eateries in town, you won't be hurting for choice at 3am. Café Bellagio (p47), America (opposite), Mr Lucky's (p56) and Bootlegger Bistro (p57) are a few après-clubbing favorites.

casual and desserts are decadent. If the line's out the door, try the nearby gourmet fast-food court.
☎ 414-3888 ⊠ Casino level, Venetian, 3355 Las Vegas Blvd S
⏰ 24/7/365 Ⓥ

Meals on Wheels
Can't stand to face the heat? **Restaurants on the Run** (☎ 735-6325, 888-447-6325; www.ontherun.cc) will deliver the goods to both sides of The Strip from a couple of dozen (mostly chain) eateries to your room for a $7 fee.

Lutèce (2, C3) $$$$
French
Impeccable modern renditions of classic gourmet French fare (sautéed foie gras with chocolate sauce) are presented in a sophisticated, austere setting. The wine cellar is top-notch and the superb seafood dishes are as sought-after as canalside seats with Strip views. Reservations essential.
☎ 414-2220 ⊠ Casino level, Venetian, 3355 Las Vegas Blvd S
⏰ 5:30-10:30pm

Pinot Brasserie (2, C3) $$$$
French-Californian
The architectural accents and the kitchen's copper pots are authentic French imports. Traditionally, however, a brasserie (Alsacean for 'brewery') was for beer and the sustenance was cheap. Here the focus is gourmet fare and fancy presentation. Don't miss the fresh-shucked shellfish and wine-tasting flights.
☎ 414-8888 ⊠ Casino level, Venetian, 3355 Las Vegas Blvd S
⏰ 11:30am-3pm & 5:30-10:30pm

Postrio (2, C3) $$$$
New American
This offshoot of Wolfgang Puck's San Francisco original features playful signature

dishes like the lobster club sandwich. Devotees can't get enough of the creative pizzas, pastas and rich desserts. The patio is designed for people-watching. Good, reasonable wine list.
☎ 796-1110 ⊠ Grand Canal Shoppes, Venetian, 3355 Las Vegas Blvd S
⏰ 11:30am-11pm, to midnight Fri & Sat

Royal Star (2, C3) $$$
Pan-Asian
Feng shui principles guided LAX airport architect Lin Wa's design of this exquisitely appointed Hong Kong-style eatery. Tableside dim sum service utilizes traditional carts, while dinner features auspicious Mandarin and Cantonese delicacies like abalone with yellow morels. Full bar.
☎ 414-1888 ⊠ Casino level, Venetian, 3355 Las Vegas Blvd S ⏰ dim sum 11am-3pm, dinner 5-11pm

Taqueria Cañonita (2, C3) $$
Mexican-Southwestern
Tacos in Italy? *Si signore*. *Gorditas, rellenos* and Yucatecan extras, like pork roasted in banana leaves, are paired with housemade corn tortillas. The exhibition kitchen and colorful Mexican tiles and folk art are visual highlights. Request

patio seating overlooking the Canal.
☎ 414-3773 ⊠ Grand Canal Shoppes, Venetian, 3355 Las Vegas Blvd S
⏰ 11am-11pm, to midnight Fri & Sat

Valentino (2, C3) $$$$
Italian
A James Beard award-winning chef, Piero Selvaggio presides over the menu of contemporary takes on classics (scads of carpaccio and truffle essence). The wine cellar of 24,000 bottles, mostly from boutique Italian vintners, is enviable, and the room is low-lit and romantic. The adjacent Grill ($$) offers wines by the glass and lighter, more affordable fare. Great tasting menus.
☎ 414-3000 ⊠ Casino level, Venetian, 3355 Las Vegas Blvd S ⏰ 5:30-11pm

Zeffirino (2, C3) $$
Italian
Housemade breads and seafood prepared with Venetian techniques are the highlights. Handcrafted furnishings accent the elegant dining room, with porch seating overlooking the canal.
☎ 414-3500 ⊠ Grand Canal Shoppes, Venetian, 3355 Las Vegas Blvd S
⏰ 11am-11pm

DOWNTOWN

Andre's (3, D4) $$$$
French-Continental
Chef André Rochat's Provençal-decorated historic 1930s home is proof that hotels don't hold a monopoly on haute cuisine. Seasonal menu highlights include roasted Provimi veal chops stuffed with king crab and wild mushroom-encrusted bison tournedos. Request patio seating and a tour of the world-class wine cellar. Dressy: resort or evening casual. Reservations essential. Also at the Monte Carlo (p51).
☎ 385-5016 🖳 www .andresfrenchrest.com ✉ 401 S 6th St 🕙 6-11pm

Binion's Ranch Steak House (3, D3) $$$$
Steakhouse
When high-rollers finish up in the poker room, they retire their Stetsons and ride the glass elevator to this classy old Vegas penthouse meatery for stunning 24th-floor views. For something more casual, hit the classic 24-hour coffee shop in the basement.
☎ 382-1600, 800-622-6468 🖳 www.binions .com ✉ Binion's Horse-show, 128 E Fremont St 🕙 6-10:30pm 🚌 108, 301, 302 🅿 free

Red Meat, After Hours
Late-night meal deals come and go, but the following are hard to beat: Binion's (above) coffee shop has a tender 10oz New York strip ($4.99) from 11pm to 7am; Mr Lucky's at the Hard Rock (p56) does an unlisted 24/7 surf-and-turf special ($7.77).

Carson Street Café (3, D3) $
American
Downtown's best 24-hour eatery slings surprisingly good grub. The Euro-style sidewalk café features sandwiches, Mexican fare, filet mignon and prime rib. For dessert, try one of the delectable sundaes. Full bar.
☎ 385-7111 🖳 www .goldennugget.com ✉ Golden Nugget, 129 E Fremont St 🕙 24/7/365 🚌 108, 301, 302 🅿 free 🚻

El Sombrero Café (3, C4) $
Mexican
Beef chili Colorado is a highlight at this humble eatery that's light years away from The Strip. It's no-smoking, family-run and intimate enough to be well-served by a lone waitress. Ask for help with the vintage jukebox and try the sweet agave-wine margaritas.
☎ 382-9234 ✉ 807 S Main St 🕙 11am-9pm Mon-Sat 🚌 108 🚻

Golden Gate Deli & Bay City Diner (3, C3) $
American-Seafood
Cheap breakfasts, graveyard steak-and-eggs, succulent porterhouse steaks and the best 99¢ shrimp cocktail in town (it's tiny – super-size

it for $2.99) are the draws at this inviting pair of eateries inside Downtown's historic San Francisco–themed hotel.
☎ 385-1906 🖳 www .goldengatecasino.com ✉ Golden Gate, 1 E Fremont St 🕙 24/7/365 🚌 108, 301, 302 🅿 free, with validation 🚻

Hugo's Cellar (3, D3) $$$$
Continental-Steakhouse
Ladies get roses on arrival at this romantic Downtown institution, a classic old Vegas gourmet room. Meals begin with an exceptional salad cart and end with chocolate-dipped fruit for dessert. In between, it's pure martinis and surf-and-turf, baby.
☎ 385-4011, 800-634-6045 🖳 www.fourqueens .com ✉ Four Queens, 202 E Fremont St 🕙 5:30-11pm 🚌 108, 301, 302 🅿 free, with validation

Pullman Bar & Grille (3, D3) $$$
Steakhouse
A well-kept secret, the Pullman features the finest Black Angus beef and seafood specialties, and a good wine list, amid gorgeous carved wood paneling. The centerpiece namesake is a 1926 Pullman train car, now a cigar lounge. Afterwards, mosey into the Triple Seven Brewpub (p59).
☎ 387-1896, 800-713-8933 🖳 www.main streetcasino.com ✉ Main Street Station, 200 N Main St 🕙 5-10:30pm Wed-Sat 🚌 108, 301, 302 🅿 free

EASTSIDE

Harrie's Bagelmania
(2, E3) $

Kosher-Deli

This kosher deli and NYC-style bagelry is the real deal, right down to the chicken in a pot and matzo ball soup. A great breakfast spot, Harrie's pulls in half the ex-Manhattanites in town.
☎ 369-3322 ✉ 855 E Twain Ave ⏲ 7am-4pm Mon-Sat 🚌 108 Ⓟ free ♿

Pamplemousse
(2, E1) $$$

French

A landmark romantic hideaway, famous for its French Riviera–style salad (a basket of fresh veggies and vinaigrette dip), appetizers like escargots and soft-shell clams, and mains like Wisconsin duckling with orange curry sauce. 'Nicely casual' dress code; jackets appreciated.
☎ 733-2066 🖥 www .pamplemousserestaurant .com ✉ 400 E Sahara Ave ⏲ 5:30-10pm Tue-Sun 🚌 301, 302 Ⓟ free

Paymon's Mediterranean Café & Hookah Lounge
(2, F4) $

Mediterranean

A great find for veggie items such as baked eggplant with fresh garlic, baba ganoush, tabouli and hummus. Carnivores should try the kebab sandwich, gyros salad or rotisserie lamb. The adjacent Hookah Lounge is a tranquil spot to chill with a water pipe and fig-flavored cocktail.

☎ 731-6030 🖥 www.paymons.com ✉ 4147 S Maryland Parkway ⏲ 11-1am Mon-Thu, 11-3am Fri & Sat, 11am-5pm Sun 🚌 109, 202 Ⓟ free Ⓥ

Siena Deli (1, B4) $

Italian-Deli

Mama mia, Siena is the best deli in town. Make a meal out of Sicilian-style flat pizza rounds, Illy espresso and the house-made tiramisu. Or grab a mouthwatering hot or cold deli sandwich. They only sell what they eat – *ho mangiato bene!*
☎ 736-8424 ✉ 2250 E Tropicana Ave ⏲ 8am-6:30pm Mon-Sat 🚌 201 Ⓟ free ♿

Hard Rock Hotel & Casino (2, D4)

The newest hard-rockin' option is Simon ($$$), featuring the updated surf-and-turf fare of Kerry Simon, who made an appearance on the *Iron Chef* on a Harley.

AJ's Steakhouse
(2, D4) $$$$

Steakhouse-Piano Bar

The Rat Pack would feel right at home in this clubby, macho chophouse. The superb steaks, filets and smooth martinis are almost overshadowed by the retro 1950s decor. Live piano jazz. Reservations essential.
☎ 693-5500 ✉ Hard Rock Hotel & Casino, 4455 Paradise Rd ⏲ 6-11pm Tue-Sat

Mr Lucky's (2, D4) $

American

A diner overlooking the casino action. The late-night comfort-food menu doesn't list the $7.77 surf-and-turf special: a juicy 8oz steak, three jumbo shrimp and your choice of starches.
☎ 693-5000 ✉ Hard Rock Hotel & Casino, 4455 Paradise Rd ⏲ 24/7/365

Nobu (2, D4) $$$

Japanese-Peruvian

Iron Chef Matasuhisa's sequel to his NYC namesake is every bite as good as the original. The beats are down-tempo…the setting pure Zen. Request sushi bar seating for a look at the samurai in action. Andean influences surface in spicy offerings like anticucho chicken skewers. The Kobe beef is suave, the cocktails creative and dessert downright decadent. Feeling flush: try the chef's special *omakase* dinner. Reservations suggested.
☎ 693-5090 ✉ Hard Rock Hotel & Casino, 4455 Paradise Rd ⏲ 6-11pm

Pink Taco (2, D4) $$

Mexican

The *comida* is Californiafied but extremely tasty at this Baja fish taco shack crossed with a low rider–themed Sunset Strip tequila bar. The margaritas are two-for-one and all the appetizers are half-price during the popular 4pm-to-7pm happy hour.
☎ 693-5000 ✉ Hard Rock Hotel & Casino, 4455 Paradise Rd ⏲ 11am-10pm, to midnight Fri & Sat, bar until 3am

WESTSIDE

Palms (2, A4)

The Palms' other varied eating options include Blue Agave ($$) for oysters; Garduño's ($$) for Mexican; N9NE ($$$) steakhouse; the Fantasy Market Buffet ($$); the 24-hour Sunrise Cafe ($) and a large fast-food court ($).

Alizé (2, A4) $$$$
French
André Rochat's (p55) top-drawer gourmet room is named after the gentle French trade wind. The panoramic views (enjoyed by every table) are stunning, just like the haute cuisine. The enormous wine-bottle tower dominates the middle of the room. Dress is resort evening-casual.
☎ 951-7000 ⌨ www .alizelv.com ✉ Top fl Palms Tower, Palms, 4321 W Flamingo Rd ⏲ 5:30-10:30pm

Little Buddha (2, A4) $$
French-Pacific Rim
An offshoot of Paris' terribly popular Buddha Bar, dishing super-fresh sushi and French-Chinese fusion. Recommended entrees include the duck confit, tempura pizza and spicy tuna tartar. The music and interior will sweep you away.
☎ 942-7778 ⌨ www .littlebuddhalasvegas .com ✉ Casino level, Palms, 4321 W Flamingo Rd ⏲ 5:30-11pm, to 12:30am Fri & Sat

Rio (2, B4)

Rio's many good eating options include Bamboleo

> ### Worth A Trip: Near McCarran Airport
> If you're killing time before a red-eye flight, try the 24-hour **Bootlegger Bistro** (1, B4; ☎ reservations 736-4939, takeout ☎ 736-7080; www.bootlegger lasvegas.com; 7700 S Las Vegas Blvd; mains $10-25), which hand-tosses the best thin-crust pizzas in town and features live nightly entertainment, a full menu round-the-clock and good graveyard specials.

($$) for Mexican; Buzio's ($$$) for seafood; the equally enticing Carnival World ($$) and Village Seafood ($$$) buffets and Rosemary's ($$$) for gourmet French-American.

All American Bar & Grille (2, B4) $$
Classic American
This casual tavern specializes in thick steaks, seafood and pork ribs, all cooked to order on a mesquite grill at the entrance of the handsome dining room. Entrees come with salad, sourdough bread and vegetables. Burgers and sandwiches are also available.
☎ 252-7767 ✉ Casino level opposite front desk, Rio, 3700 W Flamingo Rd ⏲ 11am-11pm

Antonio's (2, B4) $$$
Northern Italian
Sumptuous northern Italian cuisine in a stylish Mediterranean setting, replete with inlaid marble floors and a domed faux sky. Veal lovers should try the fork-tender osso bucco, served on a bed of saffron-infused risotto.
☎ 252-7737 ✉ Ipanema Tower,

Rio, 3700 W Flamingo Rd ⏲ 5-11pm

Fiore (2, B4) $$$$
Steakhouse-Cigar Lounge
Semiformal steakhouse with an exhibition kitchen and dramatic windows overlooking the lush pool area. Expect creative presentations of beef, veal, pork, ostrich and buffalo. Seasonal seafood highlights include grilled Maine lobster stuffed with wild mushroom risotto.
☎ 252-7777 ✉ Casino level behind high limit slot salon, Rio, 3700 W Flamingo Rd ⏲ 5-11pm

VooDoo Café & Lounge (2, B4) $$$$
American-Cajun/Creole
It's no secret that you're paying for the killer views and romantic atmosphere, but the Southern swamp-inspired cuisine is an attraction, too. Be sure to make reservations in order to avoid the lounge (p60) cover charge.
☎ 247-7923 ✉ 50th-51st fl, Masquerade Tower, Rio, 3700 W Flamingo Rd ⏲ 5-11pm, lounge to 3am, late-night menu Fri & Sat

Entertainment

If Sin City didn't invent the 24/7 lifestyle, then it's perfected it. You can catch a world-class stage show before midnight, groove to a jet-setting DJ until dawn, then catch top-notch comedy or top-fuel drag racing at noon. For its size, Vegas attracts way more than its fair share of headliners. And in recent years haute culture has blossomed.

The Strip is the obvious all-hours hotspot for drinking, comedy, shows and clubbing. Residents seek solace and let loose on the Eastside around the University of Nevada (UNLV), at strip clubs on the industrial Westside, at neighborhood bars and 'locals' casinos in the suburbs.

Three free tabloids – the *Mercury* (www.lasvegasmercury.com), *Weekly* (www.lasvegasweekly.com) and *CityLife* (www.lvcitylife.com) – hit the streets on Thursday and, when combined with the Neon section in the *Review-Journal* on Fridays, collectively offer comprehensive arts and entertainment listings.

The Thrill of Victory...Agony of Defeat
Gambling can be exhilarating, but when it comes to casinos, it's crucial to consider three words: the house advantage. For every game (except poker) the house holds a statistical 'percentage' over the gambler. This adds up to what's known as a 'long-term negative expectation' – the assurance that over the long haul the gambler will lose everything.

Our advice: approach gambling only as fee-based entertainment, not as a way to fund your children's education. Understand the game you are playing, don't bet more than you are prepared to lose and learn to walk away when you are ahead. Remember, fast money moves in two directions.

In the event that you do decide to shoot the moon, do three things first:

Take lessons Free instruction is offered at most casinos; inquire at the main cage.

Join a slot club Membership is free in the gaming equivalent of a frequent-flier program.

Get rated If playing tables, ask the pit boss to rate your play. Comps are granted based on how much you bet per hand, with $5 to $10 the minimum to qualify for free meals.

BARS, LOUNGES & BREWPUBS

Bar at Times Square (2, C5) Thirty- to fifty-somethings dig the sing-along vibe at this packed dueling piano bar. Show up early on weekends or risk waiting out in Greenwich Village. If you can't stand the queue, grab a pint nearby at Nine Fine Irishmen.
☎ 740-6969 ✉ New York-New York, 3790 Las Vegas Blvd S ⑤ $10 Fri & Sat 🕐 8-3am Sun-Thu, 8-4am Fri & Sat

Coyote Ugly (2, C5) It's a bar…a T-shirt and also a movie! A hangover-curing cereal can't be far off. The antics at this serial Southern saloon are contrived, but fun nonetheless. A rowdy mix of conventioneers and genXers worship gyrating babes in crop tops pouring shots from the bartop.
☎ 740-6330 ✉ New York-New York, 3790 Las Vegas Blvd S ⑤ $10-20 🕐 6pm-4am

Fireside Lounge at the Peppermill (2, D2) The Strip's most unlikely romantic hideaway awaits inside a retro coffee shop. Courting couples flock here for the low lighting, sunken fire pit and cozy nooks built for cuddling. Skip the food and sup a Scorpion.

☎ 735-7635 ✉ Peppermill, 2985 Las Vegas Blvd S ⑤ free 🕐 24/7/365

ghostbar (2, A4) The Palms' 55th-floor watering hole pulls in a clubby crowd with 360-degree panoramas and smart sci-fi decor.
☎ 942-7777 ✉ Palms, 4321 W Flamingo Rd ⑤ $10-20 🕐 8pm-4am

Hofbräuhaus (2, E4) Opposite the Hard Rock, this new $12 million beer hall and garden is a replica of the original in Munich. Celebrate Oktoberfest all year with imported suds, big pretzels, fair frauleins, oom-pah bands and trademark *gemütlichkeit* (congeniality).
☎ 853-3227 🖥 www .hofbrauhauslasvegas.com ✉ 4510 Paradise Rd ⑤ free 🚌 Strip shuttle 🕐 11am-dawn

Hush (2, C5) Tucked away high atop a condo complex, this lounge is best known by

a hip younger crowd for its 180-degree Strip view. The rooftop pool, private Moroccan cabañas and oversize elevated beds open up for uptempo DJ nights.
☎ 261-1000 ✉ 19th fl, Polo Towers, 3745 Las Vegas Blvd S ⑤ $5-20 🕐 8pm-4:30am

Monte Carlo Pub & Brewery (2, C5) After dark this casual industrial space is taken over by groups of hard-drinking twenty- and thirty-somethings. The pulsating dance music alternates between live and spun. More couch potato than Fred Astaire? Big-screens flash sports and rock vids.
☎ 730-7777 ✉ Monte Carlo, 3770 Las Vegas Blvd S ⑤ free, mains $9-20 🕐 11-4am

Triple Seven Brewpub (3, D3) Locals and an older casino crowd flock to this spacious Downtown spot for Monday Night Football, happy hour and graveyard specials. The sushi and oyster bar, five draught homebrews and cheap pub grub satiate all comers.
☎ 387-1896 ✉ Main Street Station, 200 N Main St ⑤ free, mains $7-20 🕐 24/7/365

Monday Night Football
Nearly every watering hole in town runs Monday night football specials. Some of the most-lively parties happen at the Hard Rock (p24), Jaguars (p67), Triple Seven Brewpub (p59) and the Palms (p25).

Special Events

Las Vegas is planning loads of events to celebrate its centennial birthday. Check www .lasvegas2005.org for a complete rundown. The Las Vegas Convention and Vistior's Authority (LVCVA; p91) maintains a schedule of annual conventions and events.

January *New Year's* – reserve a year in advance; The Strip is *the* place to celebrate

February *Mardi Gras* – fetes around town on the Saturday before Ash Wednesday

March *St Patrick's Day Parade* – downtown turns green every March 17th

Sam's Town 300 – 140,000 Nascar dads descend on the Las Vegas Motor Speedway (p69)

April *World Series of Poker* – high-rollers vie for millions at Binion's (pp22–3) and Harrah's (p24) from mid-April to mid-May

May *Cinco de Mayo* – Fremont Street Experience (p20) hosts a Mexican Independence Day celebration

June *CineVegas* – Sin City's premier film festival lights up the Palms (p25) for a week

July *High Rollers* – world's richest amateur bowling tourney at Sam's Town (1, C4)

October *Professional Bull Riders World Finals* – four days of gallopin' giddyup at Sam Boyd Stadium (p69)

November *Craftsman Truck Series* – more Nascar madness at the Las Vegas Motor Speedway (p69)

December *National Finals Rodeo* – ten days of steer wrestling at the Thomas & Mack Center (p69)

V Bar (2, C3)
Celebs, agents and glam young thangs meet and greet in this beautiful minimalist lounge. The acid jazz and low-key house music are mere accoutrements since low lighting and secluded sitting areas (and sturdy martinis) encourage intimate behavior.
☎ 414-3200 ✉ Venetian, 3355 Las Vegas Blvd S $ free, cocktails $10 ☽ 4pm-4am

Venus (2, C3)
This tiki-bar and retro-lounge combo is a favorite local hang-out. Popular for its exotic tropical cocktails, wine by the glass and close proximity to balconies overlooking The Strip. Weekly events include Wednesday

ladies nights and Saturday DJ dance parties.
☎ 414-4870 ✉ Venetian, 3355 Las Vegas Blvd S $ lounge $10-20 ☽ bar 5pm-1am Mon-Sun, lounge 9:30pm-5am Wed-Sun

VooDoo Lounge (2, B4)
The 51st-floor views from the patio are fabulous at

Rio's Masquerade Tower. The lounge boasts an extensive cocktail menu and some spirited bartender antics. There are also nightly live lounge acts. A strict dress code applies.
☎ 247-7923 ✉ Rio, 3700 W Flamingo Rd $ $10 after 8pm, free with dinner reservations (p57) ☽ 5pm-3am

Eat, drink and be merry by the Fireside at Peppermill Inn (p59)

NIGHTCLUBS & AFTER HOURS

Little expense has been spared to bring clubs at The Strip's megaresorts on par with New York and Los Angeles in the area of wildly extravagant hangouts. Surf www.vegasafter10.com for pics, VIP tips and passes, and current listings.

Beach (2, D2) Less is more and skin is in at this casual, surf-themed meat market that's popular with locals and conventioneers. The music is mostly Top 40 and ladies often drink free early on.
☎ 731-1925 ☐ www .beachlv.com ✉ 365 Convention Center Dr $ $10-20 ☽ sports bar 24/7/365, club 10pm-dawn

Body English (2, D4) The Hard Rock's elegant new Euro-style club emphasizes posh and VIP pampering. Booth reservations require one bottle ($300 minimum) per foursome, but there's a big bar upstairs. Tunes are mainstream house, hip-hop and rock.
☎ 693-4000 ☐ www .hardrockhotel.com ✉ Hard Rock, 4455 Paradise Rd $ $20 ☽ 10:30pm-4am Fri-Sun

Club Rio (2, B4) This hot and sweaty club lures a mixed young, well-dressed local singles crowd with its 30,000 sq ft, 3D laser lights and thumpin' sound system. Thursday's a hot Latin Libido frenzy, while other nights feature hip-hop and high-NRG dance music.
☎ 777-7977 ☐ www .playrio.com ✉ Rio's Scinta Showroom, 3700 W Flamingo Rd $ $10-20 ☽ 11pm-dawn Thu-Sat

Rolling Solo?

With so many newcomers and conventioneers in town, enjoying a night out alone is all too common. No worries. The singles scene is a certified USDA choice meat market; casino lounges are less cruisy. You can eat at the bar (without reservations) at most restaurants and it's easier to score a single ticket to a sold-out show than a pair. If all else fails, you can always befriend a card dealer or chat up the cocktail servers while chained to a video poker machine.

Club Seven (2, C5) The vibe at this hip, spacious lounge is DJ driven, although there's occasionally live tunes in the Stripside patio in summer. Bonuses include a fine dance floor and saddle-up sushi bar. After hours, it morphs into Alesium, a comfy spot to watch the sunrise over a Red Bull.
☎ 739-7744 ✉ 3724 Las Vegas Blvd S $ $10-30 ☽ 11pm-9am Wed-Sun

Curve (2, C4) What is 'nightlife evolved?' Ask the

small tuxedo-clad doorman. Resident DJs spin a cutting-edge progressive mix in eight ultra elegant rooms. The patio and lounging areas overlook The Strip. The chilled-out Living Room has attentive premium bottle service and spins jazz on Wednesday.
☎ 290-9582 ☐ www .curvelasvegas.com ✉ London Club at Aladdin, 3663 Las Vegas Blvd S $ $20 ☽ 10:30pm-dawn Fri & Sat, Living Room 6pm-dawn Wed-Sun

Drai's (2, C4) Ready for a scene straight outta Hollywood? Drai is an LA producer and restaurateur to the starlets. Things don't really get going until 3am, when DJs spinning progressive discs keep the fashion plates content. Dress to kill. ☎ 737-0555 ⌨ www .drais.net ✉ Barbary Coast, 3595 Las Vegas Blvd S 💲 $20 🕑 midnight-8am Wed-Sun

Foundation Room (2, C6) House of Blues' (opposite) exclusive club atop M-Bay hosts after-show parties in a luxurious dining room. Celebs like Andre Agassi hold court in the exclusive Lodge, where DJ entertainment and special events liven up the vibe. ☎ 632-7631 ⌨ www .hob.com ✉ 43rd fl, Mandalay Bay, 3950 Las Vegas Blvd S 💲 by invitation only 🕑 nightly

Light (2, C4) Intimate, sophisticated Light emphasizes socializing while professional hosts push the top-shelf bottle service – there's no bar. High-NRG dance mixes dominate the dance floor. If you want to chill, book a VIP booth. Reservations recommended. ☎ 693-8300 ⌨ www .lightlv.com ✉ Bellagio, 3600 Las Vegas Blvd S 💲 $25 🕑 10:30pm-4am Thu-Sun

Ra (2, C6) Vegas' most spectacular club is fit for the ancient Egyptian god of the sun, who inhabited the heavens by day and raged

in the underworld at night. Wednesday's Pleasuredome and Flaunt brings fashion shows, deep house and an old-school mix. Other nights feature big name house and hip-hop DJs. The dress code is fashionable and the crowd is young and sybaritic. ☎ 262-4949 ⌨ www .ralv.com ✉ Luxor, 3900 Las Vegas Blvd S 💲 $10-30 🕑 10pm-dawn Wed-Sat

Studio 54 (2, C5) Like a flawed remake of a great film, this huge three-story club fails to capture the magic that existed at New York's namesake nightspot. The decor is black, silver and industrial and the grooves are always chart toppers. Inside are mostly tourists wondering where all the glamorous people went. Thursday's Dollhouse fashion night is the best bet. ☎ 891-7254 ⌨ www .studio54lv.com ✉ MGM Grand, 3799 Las Vegas Blvd S 💲 $10-40 🕑 10pm-dawn Tue-Sat

Tabu (2, C5) It's all about stylish indulgence and sensual sophistication at MGM's latest ultralounge. DJs spin to an interactive backdrop while stunning model-hostesses mix cocktails tableside. Wednesday's Boutique night brings local designers out on the catwalk. ☎ 891-7129 ✉ MGM Grand, 3799 Las Vegas Blvd S 💲 $10-40 🕑 10pm-dawn Tue-Sun

Tangerine (2, C3) TI turns up the heat with its new orange-flavored lounge and nightclub. DJs spin pop, house and hip-hop, while burlesque dancers heat up the bartop hourly from 10:45pm to 1:45am with 15-minute quickies. The outdoor patio overlooking Sirens' Cove is the place to sit and sip while the ships cruise by during the battle royale. ☎ 992-7970 ✉ Treasure Island, 3300 Las Vegas Blvd S 💲 $20-40 🕑 10pm-4am Tue-Sat

ROCK, JAZZ & BLUES

Ease your suffering at the House of Blues

shows, even when Bob Dylan or the Rolling Stones are in town. Most shows are standing-room only, with reservable VIP balcony seats upstairs. ☎ box office 226-4650, info 693-5066 🖳 www .hardrockhotel.com ✉ Hard Rock, 4455 Paradise Rd $ $20-1000 ☽ shows from 7pm

House of Blues (2, C6)
Blues is the tip of the hog at this Mississippi Delta juke joint. Capacity is 1900, but seating is limited, so show up early if you want to take a load off. The sight lines are good and the outsider folk art decor is übercool.

☎ 632-7600 🖳 www .hob.com ✉ Mandalay Bay, 3950 Las Vegas Blvd S $ $10-100 ☽ shows from 6pm

Joint (2, D4) Concerts at this intimate venue (capacity 1400) feel like private

Sand Dollar Blues Lounge (2, B3) A few doors down from a Harley repair shop, this unpretentious club is the only one in town featuring live jazz and blues nightly. It's smoky, casual and has a nautical theme with video poker and pool tables, and draws a mixed and mostly local crowd. The Ethiopian-run Italian café next door serves good grub until late. ☎ 871-6651 ✉ 3355 Spring Mountain Rd $ $3-5 after 10pm ☽ bar 24/7, music from 10pm

Best Casino Lounge Acts
Casino-level bars at the Bellagio (p8), MGM Grand (p13), Mirage (p14), New York-New York (p16) and the Venetian (p9) host free top-notch live bands. See Sports (p6900) for information on bigger venues.

THEATER, MAGIC, CABARET & COMEDY

Big-name comedians headline the Golden Nugget (pp23–4), House of Blues (above), Hilton (pp24–5) and MGM Grand (p13).

Aladdin Theatre (2, C4)
Acts at the Aladdin Casino's upgraded 7000-seat performing-arts auditorium range from Broadway blockbusters like *Jesus Christ Superstar* to classic rock acts like Jerry Lee Lewis, and comedy kingpins such as Sinbad. ☎ 785-5055 🖳 www .aladdincasino.com

✉ Aladdin, 3667 Las Vegas Blvd S $ $25-125 ☎ box office 10am-6pm Sun-Thu, 10am-8pm Fri & Sat

Cashman Center Theatre (3, E2) Major touring productions like the *Vagina Monologues* stop at this theatre. The 1950-seat

performing-arts space is located Downtown at the Cashman Convention Center. ☎ 631-4748 ✉ 850 Las Vegas Blvd N 🚌 113 $ $20-55

Comedy Stop (2, C5)
Be sure to check out the A-list funnymen and -women cracking up the crowd at the Trop. You can find them

in the mezzanine-level cabaret during the two nightly shows.

☎ 800-829-9034
✉ Tropicana, 3801 Las Vegas Blvd S 💻 www .tropicanalv.com 💲 $15-20 🕐 8pm (nonsmoking) & 10:30pm (smoking)

The Improv (2, C3)

Harrah's features a well known and popular comedy showcase. The spotlight here is firmly cast on many of the touring stand-up headliners of the moment.

☎ 369-5111 💻 www .harrahs.com ✉ Harrah's, 3475 Las Vegas Blvd S 💲 $25 🕐 8:30pm & 10:30pm Tue-Sun

Judy Bayley Theatre (2, E4)

This theatre is the home of the UNLV's Performing Arts department and it hosts a variety of events. Everything from dance and performance art to experimental music fests and university theatrical productions.

☎ 895-2787 💻 http:// pac.nevada.edu ✉ UNLV Performing Arts Center, 4505 S Maryland Parkway 💲 $15-100 🕐 box office 10am-6pm Mon-Fri, 10am-4pm Sat 🚌 108, 109, 201

Las Vegas Little Theatre (2, A3)

Local amateur troupes have presented many 'remastered' classics like *I Hate Hamlet* at this lively community venue for three decades.

☎ 362-7996 💻 www .lvlt.org ✉ 3920 Schiff Dr 💲 $10-20

Box Offices & Info Lines

Allstate Ticketing (☎ 597-5970, 800-838-9383; www.showtickets.com) 21 outlets around town.

LVCVA hotline (☎ 892-7575, 800-332-5333; www.lasvegas24hours.com) Recorded event info.

Nevada Ticket Services (☎ 597-1588, 800-597-7469; www.lasvegastickets.com) Sold-out tickets source.

Ticketmaster (☎ 474-4000; www.ticketmaster .com) Broker for mainstream events.

Tickets2Nite (2, C5; ☎ 888-484-9264; www .tickets2nite.com; 3785 S Las Vegas Blvd) Showcase Mall half-price, same-day tickets booth.

UNLV Tickets (☎ 739-3267, 866-388-3267; www .unlvtickets.com) Source for all university events.

Le Thèâtre des Arts (2, C4)

The City of Light's 1200-seat theater presents top (if a little bit graying) inter-national recording artists, impressionists and com-edians. The likes of Natalie Cole, Dana Carvey, Elton John and Lionel Richie have all performed here with great success.

☎ 967-4567, 800-237-7469 💻 www.parislv .com ✉ Paris, 3645 Las Vegas Blvd S 💲 $60-150

PRODUCTION SHOWS

Vegas is one big show – a minimal plot production that typically includes a variety of song, dance and magic numbers. Leaving town without seeing a show is like leaving Paris without seeing Notre Dame. Kà, a new no-expenses-spared, Asian-themed Cirque du Soleil show is opening at MGM Grand (p13) in November 2004, with another water-based resident show to follow at Wynn Las Vegas (p72) in 2005.

Blue Man Group (2, C6)
A trio of nonspeaking comedic percussionists mix mind-bending audiovisual displays with juvenile but fun behavior in an odd but bemusing show. Bring a jacket: the first six rows of the audience are the recipients of catapulted Jell-O tubs, flying marshmallows and paint splattered off the tops of snare drums.
☎ 262-4400, 800-557-7428 🖳 www.blueman .com ✉ Luxor, 3900 Las Vegas Blvd S 💲 $82 & $87 🕒 7pm & 10pm daily, 7pm only Tue & Sun; inquire about additional matinees

Céline Dion: A New Day (2, C4) Cirque du Soleil maestro Franco Dragone pushed Céline to expand her limits for her new spectacular, which routinely fills Caesars' purpose-built $95-million Colosseum to capacity. She rips through 20 new ballads and greatest hits during 100 minutes, with plenty of backup from North America's biggest LED screen – and lots of hot male dancers.
☎ 731-3110, 877-423-5463 🖳 www.celine dion.com ✉ Caesars, 3570 Las Vegas Blvd S 💲 $95-242 🕒 8:30pm Wed-Sun

> ### Jubilee: Behind the Scenes
> **Bally's** (☎ 946-4567, 877-374-7469) runs one-hour backstage tours of its long-running spectacular Donn Arden's *Jubilee*. The pre-show tours ($15, $10 with show-ticket purchase) offer a sneak peek inside the lives of the showgirls and start at 2pm Monday, Wednesday and Saturday.

Folies Bergère (2, C4)
Vegas' longest-running production is a tribute to the Parisian Music Hall. Appropriately, it contains some of the most beautiful showgirls in town. The theme is 'France through the years' and the song-and-dance numbers include a fashion show, a royal ballroom number and the inevitable can-can routine.
☎ 800-829-9034 🖳 www.tropicanalv.com ✉ Tropicana, 3801 Las Vegas Blvd S 💲 $49 & $59 🕒 7:30pm (covered) & 10:30pm (topless) Mon, Wed, Thu & Sat; 8:30pm Tue & Fri 👶 over 5 at early show, over 16 othertimes

La Femme (2, C5) Za, za, zoom. The classiest topless show in town defines sexy. The 100% red room's intimate bordello feel oozes amour. Onstage, balletic dancers straight from Paris' Crazy Horse Saloon perform provocative numbers

interspersed with voyeuristic L'Art du Nu vignettes. *Zut alors* – it's a classy peep show par excellence.
☎ 891-7777, 800-929-1111 🖳 www.mgm grand.com ✉ MGM Grand, 3799 Las Vegas Blvd S 💲 $59 🕒 8pm & 10:30pm Wed-Mon

Mystère (2, C3)
Cirque du Soleil director Franco Dragone does for theater what Dali did for painting. His evocative celebration of life begins with a pair of babies making their way in a world filled with strange creatures. A misguided clown's humorous antics are interspersed with acrobats, aerialists and dancers performing one spectacular feat of strength and agility after another.
☎ 894-7722, 800-392-1999 🖳 www.cirquedu soleil.com ✉ Treasure Island, 3300 Las Vegas Blvd S 💲 $95, limited seats for $60 🕒 7pm & 10pm Wed-Sun

O (2, C4)
Cirque du Soleil's original venture into aquatic theater is truly a spectacular feat of imagination. 'Eau' (French for water) is 3-D surrealism. A talented international cast – performing in, on and above the precious liquid – surveys drama through the ages.
☎ 693-7722, 888-488-7111 ⬚ www.cirquedu soleil.com ✉ Bellagio, 3600 Las Vegas Blvd S 💲 $99-150 🕑 7:30pm & 10:30pm Wed-Sun

Rita Rudner (2, C5)
The comedien, whose trademark is telling stories and delivering one-liners with soft-spoken naiveté, delivers a real kick in the pants. Her shrewd observations about life are a hoot and the intimate theater

---

Siegfried & Roy

Prior to the near-fatal mauling of Roy by one of his trained white tigers in October 2003, the dynamic illusionist duo had been wowing audiences for decades. Sadly, there are no plans for their show to return, but you can still see the tigers at the Mirage (p14) and monitor Roy's recovery via www .siegfriedandroy.com.

(425 seats) lends itself well to her shtick.
☎ 740-6815, 866-606-7111 ⬚ www.ritafunny .com ✉ New York-New York, 3790 Las Vegas Blvd S 💲 $60 🕑 8pm Mon-Thu, 9pm Fri & Sat

Zumanity (2, C5)
Billed as 'another side of Cirque du Soleil,' the Human Zoo shares the energized pulse, contorted acrobatics and flirtatious eroticism of the troupe's other risk-

taking resident Strip shows. So what's the hook that's made it the hottest ticket in town? Maybe it's the curvilinear thrust stage, uninhibited costumes by Thierry Mugler...or the romantic red loveseats reserved for couples?
☎ 740-6815, 800-963-9364 ⬚ www.zuman ity.com ✉ New York-New York, 3790 Las Vegas Blvd S 💲 $65-125 🕑 7:30pm & 10:30pm Fri-Tue

CLASSICAL MUSIC, OPERA & DANCE

Watch for the debut of a new special-effects rendition of Andrew Lloyd Webber's *Phantom of the Opera* – complete with an onstage lake and an exploding replica of the Paris Opera House chandelier – in a purpose-built $25 million theater at the Venetian (p9) in early 2006.

Las Vegas Philharmonic (2, E4) This 80-piece orchestra performs at UNLV's Artemus Ham Concert Hall and around town at casino grand openings.
☎ 895-2787 ⬚ www .lvphil.com ✉ UNLV Performing Arts Center, 4505 S Maryland Parkway 💲 $25-66 🕑 shows 8pm 🚌 108, 109, 201 🅿 $2

Nevada Ballet Theatre (2, E4) Nevada's only

professional dance company presents both classical and contemporary performances year-round at a variety of venues, primarily at UNLV's Judy Bayley Theatre.
☎ 243-2623 ⬚ www .nevadaballet.com ✉ UNLV Performing Arts Center, 4505 S Maryland Pkwy 💲 $20-65 🕑 call for schedule

UNLV Performing Arts Center (2, E4) UNLV hosts over 600 events on three

stages. The 1870-seat Artemus Ham Concert Hall has great acoustics while the 550-seat Judy Bayley Theatre accommodates everything from ballet to experimental music fests. The intimate Black Box Theatre presents smaller theatrical productions.
☎ 895-2787 ⬚ http:// pac.nevada.edu ✉ 4505 S Maryland Parkway 💲 $10-80 🕑 box office 10am-6pm Mon-Fri, 10am-4pm Sat

STRIP CLUBS

Vegas is the original adult Disneyland. Prostitution may be illegal, but there are plenty of places offering the illusion of sex on demand.

Girls of Glitter Gulch (3, D3) As you experience Fremont St (p20), you can't help but notice this topless joint that Downtown boosters wish would just go away. Inside you'll find friendly dancers and a mostly tourist crowd; unescorted women are welcome.
☎ 385-4774 ✉ 20 E Fremont $ free; 2 drink minimum, drinks $7-9 🕐 1pm-4am 🚌 108, 301, 302 P $1 self parking at Fremont Experience garage

Jaguars (2, B2) This large, opulent topless gentleman's club is the most refined cat on Sin City's adult entertainment block. There's a sushi bar, popular VIP room and Monday Night Football specials.
☎ 732-1116 🖥 www .jaguarslv.cc ✉ 3355 S Procyon Ave $ $20 after 8pm 🕐 4:30pm-4am

Olympic Garden (3, C5) The OG wins high marks from topless-club aficionados – and the nickname

Bachelor & Bachelorette Party Venues
Looking to organize one last wild night out? Besides strip clubs (below), the Hard Rock (p24), Palms (p25) and Rio (pp25–6) cater to the on-the-verge crowd.

Party hard at Little Buddha (p57) and then party harder

'Silicone Valley' from the competition. Up to 50 dancers work at any given time, thus there's something to please everyone. Studs strip upstairs Wednesday through Sunday.
☎ 385-9361 🖥 www .ogvegas.com ✉ 1531 Las Vegas Blvd S $ $20 🕐 24/7/365

Sapphire (2, C2) Owned by Olympic Garden and

billed as the 'world's largest adult entertainment complex,' this 10,000-sq-ft complex is the most grown-up topless joint in town, with a stable of 6000 entertainers and VIP skyboxes overlooking the showroom.
☎ 796-6000 🖥 www .saphirelasvegas.com ✉ 3025 S Industrial Rd $ $20 after 6pm 🕐 24/7/365

Girls Just Wanna Have Fun
The dancers at Rio's (pp25–6) 400-seat **Chippendales theater** ($35-45; 🕐 10pm) seem more concerned with basking in the spotlight than giving the girls a feel. Private sky boxes, a spacious cocktail lounge and plush bathroom with a 'gossip pit' are the icing on the hunky cake. At Excalibur (p23), you can touch the lovely lads of **Thunder Down Under** ($35-45; 🕐 8:30pm & 10:30pm), who provide nonstop fun and flirting…a bachelorette party must! The down-and-dirty Men of Olympus strut their stuff upstairs Wednesday through Sunday at the Olympic Garden (above).

Jennifer L Leo

CINEMAS

Check **Moviefone** (☎ 222-3456; www.moviefone.com) for show times, trailers and music listings.

Brenden IMAX 14 (2, A4)
The swankest off-Strip movie-plex is fitted with IMAX and Lucasfilm THX digital sound, plus stadium seating for superior sightlines.
☎ 507-4849 🖥 www.brendentheatres.com ✉ Palms, 4321 W Flamingo Rd 💲 matinee $9/6

Crown Neonopolis 14 (3, D3) Vegas' newest theater is also the cheapest. All 14 screens sport digital

THX sound and high-backed, stadium-style seating.
☎ 383-9600 🖥 www.crowntheatres.com ✉ 450 E Fremont St 💲 matinee $8/5

Luxor IMAX Theatre (2, C6) Luxor's theater projects onto a seven-story, wall-mounted – rather than curved overhead – screen, but the images are 10 times more detailed than conventional cinemas. With only 312 seats, you're pretty

close to the action.
☎ 262-4555, 800-557-7428 ✉ Luxor, 3900 Las Vegas Blvd S 💲 $10-15

UA Showcase 8 (2, C5)
First-run flicks fill the bill at the Showcase Mall's newish theater where all screens are blessed with digital sound.
☎ 740-4511, 222-3456 (Moviefone) ext 759 🖥 www.regmovies.com ✉ Showcase Mall, 3769 Las Vegas Blvd S 💲 matinee $9/6

GAY & LESBIAN LAS VEGAS

East of The Strip and just west of the UNLV campus, the Fruit Loop triangle is an island of flamboyance in a sea of straightness and home to Vegas' queer community. See www.gaylasvegas.com, www.outlasvegas.com or www.outinlasvegas.com for info on Sin City's active scene.

Apollo Spa (2, E1; ☎ 650-9191; www.apollospa.com; Commercial Center, 953 E Sahara Ave) is a steamy men's health club. Stop by **Get Booked** (2, E5; ☎ 737-7780; www.getbookedlasvegas.com; 4640 S Paradise Rd) for party invites. For more details, see p87.

Blue Moon Resort (2, C1)
At Sin City's first gay, cloth-ing-optional getaway, it's all about the pool and parties. Rates ($89 to $199) include adult programming and use of the sultry steam room.
☎ 361-9099, 866-798-9194 🖥 www.bluemoonlv.com ✉ 2651 Westwood Dr

Buffalo (2, E5) Cruisy Levis- and leather-clad boyz hang at this bar with pool tables, beer busts and plenty of tough-looking but friendly fellows out for a good time.

☎ 733-8355 ✉ 4640 Paradise Rd 💲 free 🕒 24/7/365 🚌 108, 203

Free Zone (2, E5) Every night is a party at this hang-out. Tuesday is ladies night, Thursday is boyz night and Friday and Saturday nights feature What a Drag cabaret.
☎ 794-2300 ✉ 610 E Naples Dr 💲 free 🕒 24/7/365 🚌 108, 203

Gipsy (2, E5) By all ac-counts, this is the premier gay dance club in town.

There's always a party and a daily happy hour.
☎ 731-1919 ✉ 4605 S Paradise Rd 💲 $5-10 after 10pm 🕒 9pm-late 🚌 108, 203

Goodtimes (1, B4) A men's club where conversa-tion rules, but there's a steel dance floor. Happy hour runs 5pm to 7pm daily, with a legendary Monday liquor bust from midnight to 3am.
☎ 736-9494 ✉ Liber-ace Museum, 1775 E Tropicana Ave 💲 free 🕒 24/7/365 🚌 201

SPORTS

Although Vegas doesn't have any professional sports franchises, it's a very sports-savvy town. Handicapping is one of the most popular activities. There are no fewer than five **all-sports radio stations** (p90) and you can wager on just about anything at race and sports books.

World-class **boxing** draws fans from all around the globe. UNLV Runnin' Rebels **college football**, **baseball** and **basketball** teams enjoy a strong local following. The minor-league Las Vegas Wranglers (www .lasvegaswranglers.com) **ice-hockey** team faces off October to April at the Orleans Arena. **Auto racing** at Las Vegas Motor Speedway (see boxed text below) is enormously popular.

Sports & Concert Venues

Las Vegas Motor Speedway (1, C2; ☎ 644-4444, 800-644-4444; www.lvms .com; 7000 Las Vegas Blvd N) – 125,000 seats: Nascar, Indy racing, drag racing, dirt track

Mandalay Bay Events Center (2, C6; ☎ 877-632-7800; www.mandalaybay.com; 3950 Las Vegas Blvd S) – 12,000 seats: boxing, headliner concerts, bull riding

MGM Grand Garden Arena (2, C5; ☎ 877-880-0880; www.mgmgrand.com; 3799 Las Vegas Blvd S) – 17,000 seats: boxing, motorsports, mega concerts, tennis

Orleans Arena (2, A5; ☎ 888-234-2334; www.orleansarena.com; Orleans, 4500 W Tropicana Ave) – 9000 seats: boxing, hockey, motorsports, concerts

Sam Boyd Stadium (1, C4; ☎ 888-464-2468; www.samboydstadium.com; 7000 E Russell Rd) – 40,000 seats: UNLV college football, motorsports, concerts

Thomas & Mack Center (2, E5; ☎ 895-3900; www.thomasandmack.com; UNLV, 4505 S Maryland Parkway) – 19,000 seats: rodeo, WWF wrestling, concerts, college basketball, motorsports

Sleeping

With more than 130,000 guestrooms, there's no shortage of places to stay in the Vegas Valley. Options range from filthy fleapits east of Downtown to exquisite penthouse suites overlooking The Strip. Accommodations range from $15 per night at a hostel to $10,000 for a private self-contained villa with butler service at one of The Strip's ritzy megaresorts.

Occupancy rates hover around 90% and rates fluctuate wildly according to demand. While the price of poker has risen steeply in recent years, midweek tariffs are up to 50% lower than on weekends. Contact the Las Vegas Convention & Visitors Authority (LVCVA; p91) about last-minute specials and for a current listing of convention dates.

Many properties lure customers during slow periods with discounted room rates – ask if they are 'inclusive' to avoid hidden charges. These loss-leader tariffs are advertised online and in Sunday travel sections of major newspapers. Remember that Strip properties can offer rooms for the same price as a dumpy Downtown joint since they make their bucks in gaming areas, whereas the dumpy joint doesn't have a casino to recoup its losses.

Room Rates

Price ranges indicate midweek (Sunday to Thursday) rack rates for one night in a standard double during nonholiday, nonconvention periods. Rates can triple during big conventions and even quadruple for major holidays like Valentine's Day and New Year's Eve.

Deluxe	from $299
Luxury	$200–299
Top End	$126–199
Mid-Range	$75–125
Budget	under $75

Sumptuous lobby of the Venetian

Whatever you do, don't arrive without a reservation, at least for the first night. You'd be amazed how often every standard room in town is occupied. During the biggest conventions, even Laughlin (75 miles away) is booked solid. If you simply turn up looking for a room, you may be stuck with an overpriced two-bedroom suite. The time-tested low-roller strategy is to stay in less-luxurious places next to where you plan to spend your time. However, if you've got the cash, this is the place to splash out in style.

Hotel Bookies

Booking agencies, which reserve rooms in bulk and pass on volume discounts, are most useful when everything is supposedly sold out. The **Las Vegas Convention & Visitors Authority** (LVCVA; ☎ 800-332-5333) can also help out in a pinch.

- **Hotels.com** (☎ 800-246-8357; www.hotels.com)
- **National Reservations Bureau** (☎ 800-638-5553; www.nrbinc.com)

DELUXE

Luxury comes cheaper here than almost anywhere else in the world. If you splash cash around the casino, expect to be comped a suite. Impeccable service, 24/7 concierge pampering and expedited airport check-in are standard. Suites at most Top End hotels fall into the Deluxe category.

Bellagio (2, C4) If anything in Vegas is truly 'spectacular,' this luxe five-diamond destination is it. Lavish bathrooms feature marble, plush robes and deep tubs. Guestrooms are styled out with artwork and views of the lush grounds. The new Spa Tower suites elevate luxury to a new level.
☎ 693-7111, 888-987-6667 ☐ www.bellagio.com ✉ 3600 Las Vegas Blvd S Ⓜ Bally's & Paris 🚠 to Monte Carlo ✗ see pp47–8

Four Seasons (2, C6) Private elevators whisk guests away to the exclusive rooms on Mandalay Bay's (p72) 35th through 39th floors. The nongaming resort emphasizes comfort, quiet and

concierge coddling. In-room Internet, a full-service spa and twice-daily housekeeping seal the deal.
☎ 632-5000, 877-632-5000 ☐ www.four seasons.com/lasvegas ✉ Mandalay Bay, 3960 Las Vegas Blvd S 🚠 to Luxor & Excalibur ✗ see pp50–1 🚸 under 18 free

THEhotel (2, C6) Relax: from THE moment you enter THE lobby adjacent to Mandalay Bay (p72), you feel a world away from THE Strip's hustle and bustle. THE expansive suites boast Internet, bars, plasma TVs, living areas and NYC chic decor. Special business-friendly suites are adjacent to THE convention center. Twenty nonsuite rooms are

slightly less expensive.
☎ 632-7777, 877-632-7800 ☐ www.mandalaybay.com ✉ Mandalay Bay, 3950 Las Vegas Blvd S 🚠 to Luxor & Excalibur ✗ see pp50–1

Venetian (2, C3) Fronted by canals and graceful bridges, the Venetian's 'standard' rooms are anything but. In fact, they are the largest and most luxurious in town, with oversized baths and canopy-draped beds. The new Venezia Tower has a private pool and exclusive concierge level.
☎ 414-1000, 888-283-6423 ☐ www.venetian.com ✉ 3355 Las Vegas Blvd S Ⓜ Harrah's & Imperial Palace ✗ see pp53–4

TOP END

Most standard rooms at The Strip's megaresorts fall into this range. Expect luxurious bathrooms with marble tubs, high-tech bells and whistles and attention lavished on decor.

Bally's (2, C4) Two blissfully theme-free towers house spacious rooms and suites. Rooms have sofas and are pleasantly decorated. Extras include a health club, tennis courts and poolside cabanas.
☎ 739-4111, 888-742-9248 ☐ www.ballyslv.com ✉ 3645 Las Vegas Blvd S Ⓜ Bally's & Paris ✗ see p46

Caesars Palace (2, C4) Decadence still reigns. Caesars' rooms are some of the most luxurious in town. A new all-suite tower overlooking the huge pool complex will debut in 2005.
☎ 731-7110, 877-427-7243 ☐ www .caesarspalace.com ✉ 3570 Las Vegas Blvd S Ⓜ Flamingo & Caesars ✗ see pp48–9

Hard Rock (2, D4) Rock on. Everything about this intimate hotel suggests stardom. Suites have stereos, large-screen TVs, WiFi and jet tubs. The action revolves around the pool area, with a sexy sandy beach.
☎ 693-5000, 800-473-7625 ☐ www.hardrockhotel.com ✉ 4455 Paradise Rd 🚌 free Strip shuttle ✗ see p56

A World-Class Wynner

Impresario Steve Wynn, best known for developing the Mirage and Bellagio, is scheduled to open a new resort in April 2005, in the heart of The Strip. It's scheduled to debut with a 50-story hotel tower, 2,700 suites, Maserati and Ferrari dealerships and The Strip's only 18-hole golf course. The risqué, Tony award–winning play *Avenue Q* will run in a $40 million purpose-built theater. The theme? Elegance. Finally, a signal that Vegas is returning to its classy roots.

Las Vegas Hilton (2, E2)

The decor at this conventioneer's hotel can only be described as upscale-contemporary American. Digs are spacious, with automated drapes and deeper-than-usual tubs.
☎ 732-5111, 888-732-7117 🖥 www.lvhilton.com ✉ 3000 Paradise Rd Ⓜ Hilton ✕ Andiamo, Benihana, The Buffet, Garden of the Dragon, Hilton Steakhouse, Margarita Grille, Paradise Cafe, Tera Sushi

Mandalay Bay (2, C6)

The eclectic South Seas theme persists throughout the rooms. Amenities include luxurious bathrooms. Many guests feel that it's worth staying here just for the pool complex.
☎ 632-7777, 877-632-7800 🖥 www.mandalay bay.com ✉ 3950 Las Vegas Blvd S 🚝 to Luxor & Excalibur ✕ see pp50–1

MGM Grand (2, C5)

There's plenty to choose from at the world's largest hotel, but is bigger better? Yes and no. The suites can be a bargain. It's the casino and entertainment options that make it shine.
☎ 891-7777, 877-880-0880 🖥 www.mgm grand.com ✉ 3799 Las Vegas Blvd S Ⓜ MGM Grand ✕ see p51

Mirage (2, C3)

Rooms here are elegant but smaller than most, and all have marble entryways. If space is a concern, upgrade to a suite – you can do better elsewhere, but the central location is tough to beat.
☎ 791-7111, 800-374-9000 🖥 www.mirage.com ✉ 3400 Las Vegas Blvd S 🚝 to Treasure Island ✕ see p51

Monte Carlo (2, C5)

It's hardly Monaco, but European style permeates the rooms. The swimming complex is cool (with a river and a wave pool) and the spa is something to behold.
☎ 730-7777, 888-529-4828 🖥 www.monte-carlo.com ✉ 3770 Las Vegas Blvd S 🚝 to Bellagio ✕ see pp51–2

Palms (2, A4)

Off-Strip and originally aimed at young locals, the post – *Real World* Palms now attracts a flashier MTV-influenced crowd. Rooms are generous with tech-savvy amenities. The playpen suites are tailored for bachelor and bachelorette parties (p67).
☎ 942-7777, 866-942-7770 🖥 www.palms.com ✉ 4321 W Flamingo Rd 🚌 free Strip shuttle ✕ see p57

Paris (2, C4)

Rooms at this Hotel de Ville replica are comfortable with armoires enhancing the Gallic feel. Rates climb for upper-floor rooms with views. Above all else, the location is ace.
☎ 946-7000, 877-796-2096 🖥 www.parislv.com ✉ 3655 Las Vegas Blvd S Ⓜ Bally's & Paris ✕ see pp52–3

Rio (2, B4)

The all-suite Rio is a great deal – if you don't mind being off-Strip. Most rooms boast separate vanity and dressing areas and a huge TV. Some rooms are windowless.
☎ 777-7777, 877-746-7153 🖥 www.playrio.com ✉ 3700 W Flamingo Rd 🚌 202; free Strip shuttle ✕ see p57

Treasure Island (2, C3)

Unless you really dig the Caribbean vibe, save your suite money for somewhere classier. The elegant hideaway theme mercifully fades away inside TI's grown-up rooms.
☎ 894-7111, 800-288-7206 🖥 www.treasure island.com ✉ 3300 Las Vegas Blvd S 🚝 to the Mirage ✕ Buccaneer Bay, Canter's Deli, Francesco's, Isla, Steak House, Dishes buffet

MID-RANGE

Stepping down in price doesn't necessitate forfeiting amenities. Less staff, smaller rooms or a less-prime location often account for lower rates.

Flamingo (2, C4) It attracts flocks of faithful for two good reasons: price and location. The tropical-themed rooms are tiny. The Four Corners location, however, trumps the downsides.
☎ 733-3111, 888-308-8899 🖳 www.flamingo lasvegas.com ✉ 3555 Las Vegas Blvd S 🅼 Caesars & Flamingo 🍽 Conrad's Steakhouse, Hamada of Japan, Margaritaville 🛉

Golden Nugget (3, D3) The elegant, ample rooms are good value, while the apartments are truly unique. A spa and fitness center round out this class act.
☎ 385-7111, 800-846-5336 🖳 www.golden nugget.com ✉ 129 E Fremont St 🚌 301, 302 🍽 Buffet, Carson Street Café, Lillie Langtry's, Stefano's, ZAX

Luxor (2, C6) Luxor's rooms are one of the best mid-range deals. The newer tower often has better views. Indulge with a treatment at the 24-hour Oasis spa (p25).
☎ 262-4000, 888-777-0188 🖳 www.luxor.com ✉ 3900 Las Vegas Blvd S 🚃 to Excalibur & Mandalay Bay 🍽 Fusia,

Isis, Luxor Steakhouse, Pharaoh's Pheast Buffet, Sacred Sea Room 🛉

Main Street Station (3, D3) The 406 rooms are bright and cheery. The 17-floor tower features marble foyers and hallways. Suites are sweet, but reserved for high-rollers.
☎ 387-1896, 800-465-0711 🖳 www.mainstreet casino.com ✉ 200 N Main St 🚌 shuttle to/from Sam's Town & upper Strip 🍽 Garden Court Buffet, Pullman Grille (p55), Triple Seven Brewpub (p59)

New York-New York (2, C5) As in NYC, elbow room is lacking in the amenity-packed rooms. Avoid noisy lower-level rooms facing Manhattan Express (p21).
☎ 740-6969, 866-815-4365 🖳 www.nynyhotel casino.com ✉ 3790 Las Vegas Blvd S 🅼 MGM Grand 🍽 see p52 🛉

Stratosphere (2, D1) The main feature at Stratosphere is its distance from the action. Size is average but the decor is fetching. A mandatory $5 resort fee includes free Tower admission.

☎ 800-998-6937, 888-236-7495 🖳 www.strato spherehotel.com ✉ 2000 Las Vegas Blvd S 🍽 Courtyard Buffet, Fellini's Ristorante, Hamada Asian Village, Roxy's Diner, Top of the World (p53) 🛉

Tropicana (2, C5) Famous since 1957, the Trop is still going strong. The Island Tower retains a kitschy Polynesian theme. Most of the rooms have big windows but are cramped. The pool complex keep things cool.
☎ 739-2222, 888-826-8767 🖳 www.tropicana lv.com ✉ 3801 Las Vegas Blvd S 🅼 MGM Grand 🍽 Calypsos, Island Buffet, Legends Deli, Mizuno's (p53), Pietro's, Savanna Steakhouse 🛉

Viva Las Vegas Villas (3, C5) Tying the knot? This wedding wonderland is the most inviting place between Downtown and The Strip. Breakfast is served in a 1950s diner with free Internet. Watch weddings live online!
☎ 384-0771, 800-574-4450 🖳 www.vivalas vegasvillas.com ✉ 1205 Las Vegas Blvd S 🚌 301, 302

Convention Hotels

Conventioneers are best off within walking distance of their venue. For the Las Vegas Convention Center, the Las Vegas Hilton (opposite) is close. The Stardust (p26), Riviera, Sahara (p26) and Courtyard Marriott are a short cab ride away. The Venetian (p9) is linked to the Sands Convention Center, and Treasure Island (p12) is nearby.

BUDGET

Barbary Coast (2, C4)
With rooms from $40 smack bang mid-Strip, the Barbary is the Strip's worst kept secret. The charming decor in the casino transfers seamlessly to the basic rooms. Given the value and location, it's often tough to secure a bed.
☎ 737-7111, 888-227-2279 🖳 www .barbarycoastcasino.com ✉ 3595 Las Vegas Blvd S Ⓜ Flamingo & Caesars ✖ Drai's (p62), Michael's (p46), Victorian Room (p46) ⚓

Circus Circus (2, D2)
Most standard rooms at this popular family favorite have sofas and balconies. Suites come in varying shapes and sizes. The decor is tasteful and most of the rooms are nonsmoking. Avoid the motel-style Manor rooms out back.
☎ 734-0410, 877-224-7287 🖳 www.circus circus.com ✉ 2880 Las Vegas Blvd S ✖ Steak House (p49) ⚓ under 18 free

Excalibur (2, C5) For better or worse, the relentless Arthurian motif doesn't end in the casino. The two towers house 4000 plus rooms, all wallpapered to resemble a castle. Upsides include nonsmoking, family-friendly rooms, wheelchair-friendly doors and Jacuzzi suites.
☎ 597-7777, 877-750-5464 🖳 www.excalibur .com ✉ 3050 Las Vegas Blvd S 🚍 to Luxor & Mandalay Bay Ⓜ MGM Grand

✖ Regale, Sir Galahad's Pub ⚓ under 18 free

Gold Coast (2, B4)
The standard rooms here are unremarkable, but they won't leave you feeling squeezed. You can do better elsewhere, but some folks prefer the tranquil off-Strip location.
☎ 367-7111, 888-402-6278 🖳 www .goldcoastcasino.com ✉ 4000 W Flamingo Rd 🚍 free Strip shuttle ✖ Arriva, Cortez Room, Monterey Room, Ping Pang Pong, Ports O' Call Buffet ⚓ free child care

Orleans (2, A5) The pretty French provincial–decorated rooms are quite good value and also include separate sitting, dining and bedroom areas. There's also a spa, a fitness center, an arcade, child care and the best bowling alley.
☎ 365-7111, 800-675-3267 🖳 www.orleans casino.com ✉ 4500 W Tropicana Ave 🚍 201; airport & Strip shuttles ✖ Big Al's Oyster Bar, Canal Street, Don Miguel's, French Market Buffet, Koji, Prime Rib Loft, Sazio ⚓ cribs & child care, under 18 free

Traveling with Children

Bad news: most Strip megaresorts don't cater to kids and a few actually discourage them. Notable exceptions include Circus Circus (left), Excalibur (below), and the Four Seasons (p71), where kids under 18 stay for free. See p29 for babysitting-service details.

Beware the clowns at Circus Circus

About Las Vegas

HISTORY

What history, you ask. Looking around, you are to be forgiven. Unlike the rest of the ruin-laden US Southwest, traces of early history are scarce.

Contrary to Hollywood legend, there was much more at the dusty crossroads than a gambling parlor and some tumbleweeds the day that mobster Ben 'Bugsy' Siegel (p23) rolled into this one-horse settlement and erected a glamorous, tropical-themed casino under the searing sun.

Uto-Aztecan–speaking Paiute people inhabited the Las Vegas Valley for a millennium before the Spanish Trail was blazed through the last area to be explored by Anglos. Travelers bestowed the name 'las vegas' (the meadows) on the little life-saving oasis in the middle of the Mojave Desert.

Taming the Desert

The completion of a railroad linking Salt Lake City to Los Angeles in 1902 created the need for a division point for crew changes. Thus Las Vegas, then known as Ragtown, entered the modern era. A railroad strike in 1922 left Vegas economically stranded again, but the Boulder (later named Hoover) Dam project wasn't far off, bringing badly needed water and economic stimulus.

Hoover Dam, Gambling & Divorce

Federally sponsored construction by the Bureau of Reclamation in the late 1920s stimulated another economic boom; the legalization of gambling in 1931 carried Vegas through the Great Depression. Bookmakers fleeing Los Angeles and Tijuana, Mexico, flocked to the newly minted Sin City. Lax divorce requirements, quickie weddings, legal prostitution and championship boxing bouts proved safe bets for local boosters. New Deal dollars kept flowing into Southern Nevada's coffers right through WWII.

Nevada's Nuclear Desert

The US government stopped exploding nuclear bombs underground at the Nevada Test Site in 1992, but a nuclear future still looms large for state residents. In 1998, a US Department of Energy report, which took 18 years and over $5 billion to research, recommended Yucca Mountain as the best location for the nation's only long-term radioactive nuclear-waste repository.

Did we say long-term? The proposed site, which would eventually hold 77,000 tons of used spent nuclear fuel, would remain deadly for 300,000 years. In that time, the earth itself may experience an ice age, and Yucca Mountain, currently one of the driest and most remote places in the lower 48 states, may no longer be a desert. Anyone care to predict the weather a few millennia from now?

Nevada officials, including Vegas mayor Oscar Goodman, fought the proposed waste dump but in 2002 congress approved the Yucca Mountain Project proposal by President W Bush, whose Republican party receives millions in campaign contributions from the nuclear industry. Waste storage is scheduled to begin as early as 2010.

Atomic Age

WWII brought a huge air-force base and big bucks, plus a paved highway to LA. Soon after, the Cold War justified the Nevada Test Site. It proved to be the textbook case of any publicity is good publicity: monthly above-ground atomic blasts shattered casino windows Downtown, while the city's official Miss Mushroom Cloud mascot promoted atomic everything in tourism campaigns. Concerns about the radioactive fallout from the nuclear era are mirrored in the current battle over a proposed $49.3 billion high-level nuclear waste repository 100 miles northeast of Las Vegas at Yucca Mountain (p75).

Golden Age

A building spree sparked by the Flamingo in 1946 led to mob-backed tycoons upping the glitz ante. Hotels from this era that have dodged implosion include Binion's, the Sahara, Stardust and the Riviera. Big-name entertainers like Frank Sinatra, Liberace and Sammy Davis Jr arrived on stage at the same time as topless French showgirls (p24). Construction of the convention center in 1960 capped off a prosperous era.

The high-profile purchase of the Desert Inn in 1966 by the billionaire Howard Hughes gave the gambling industry a much-needed patina of legitimacy in the face of mounting bad publicity from highly publicized organized-crime links. Spearheaded by Hughes's spending spree, corporate ownership of casinos blossomed and publicly traded companies bankrolled a building bonanza in the late 1960s and early '70s. The debut of the MGM Grand in 1993 signaled the dawn of the era of the corporate 'megaresort.'

The Show Must Go On

Casinos have only dimmed their marquee lights on six occasions. The first time was for three hours in 1963, following the assassination of President John F Kennedy. Casinos shut their doors again in 1968, after an assassin's bullet claimed the life of Reverend Martin Luther King Jr.

The casinos remained open for business when Sammy Davis Jr died of throat cancer in 1990, but their marquees went blank in unison for 10 minutes. Lights were dimmed again for two more Rat Pack brothers – when Dean Martin succumbed to acute respiratory failure in 1995, and when Frank Sinatra was silenced by a heart attack in 1998.

The most recent moment of silence came after the tragic 9/11 attacks on NYC's World Trade Center.

Las Vegas Today & Tomorrow

An oasis in the middle of a final frontier, Sin City continues to exist chiefly to satisfy the needs and desires of visitors. Hosting over 35 million visitors a year, Las Vegas is the engine of the US's fastest-growing metro area and the last port of opportunity for countless people seeking their fortune. Best of all for shareholders, there seems to be no end in sight to the growth of the progressive jackpot at the world's best-known tourist destination, barring an environmental meltdown.

Meanwhile, as slots go cashless and omnipotent surveillance goes digital, 'Spin' City approaches the Orwellian dream-nightmare. It doesn't matter whether you love Vegas or hate it, everyone really ought to experience the world's first 21st-century city for themselves.

ENVIRONMENT

Las Vegas is an environmentalist's nightmare, the antithesis of a naturalist's vision of America. It's also a gateway to some of the Southwest's most spectacular natural attractions.

> **Did You Know?**
> - The entire Clark County has 1.65 million residents
> - Annual gambling revenue nears $8 billion
> - Only 13% of Vegas' visitors do not gamble
> - The Vegas Valley has over 130,000 hotel rooms
> - The annual average income in Clark County is $34,058
> - In 2003, Clark County averaged 5266 new residents per month
> - Las Vegas' cost of living is lower than any other US metro area

Water usage is of chief concern. The city receives the vast majority of its water from the Colorado River, which feeds Lake Mead. Projections suggest that the Las Vegas Valley may exhaust its entire water supply by 2010. What will happen when the aquifers run dry is anyone's guess.

Water pollution is another big problem. Lake Mead receives partially treated effluent pumped back by Vegas' sewage plants. Even more alarming is that more partially treated effluent is entering the lake than ever before, and the volume of water leaving the lake exceeds the amount entering it.

Air pollution is an equally vexing topic: the valley is fringed by mountains that trap hazardous particulates, and the city is in near-constant violation of EPA air-quality standards.

GOVERNMENT & POLITICS

Wary of the pitfalls of centralized power, Vegas adopted the council-manager form of government in 1994. Four elected members and a mayor serve four-year terms. A city manager runs day-to-day operations.

In a major blow to official public relations efforts to clean up Sin City's image, voters elected long-time Mafia consigliere Oscar Goodman as mayor in 1999. Goodman gained fame as a defense attorney for goodfellas Frank 'Lefty' Rosenthal and Tony 'The Ant' Spillotro. He caught the voters' fancy with a populist platform calling for developers to pay fees to help solve urgent traffic and pollution woes. Goodman's achievements include getting his mug on limited-edition chips, endorsing a brand of gin for $100,000 (donated to charities) and hosting 'Martini with the Mayor' nights. Viva Las Vegas! He was re-elected with 86% of the vote in 2003.

ECONOMY

Tourism drives southern Nevada's economy. Over 35 million tourists a year spend an average of four days in Vegas. Approximately half of the city's workforce is employed in service industries.

Gaze down on the Strip from the Stratosphere

Eighty percent of visitors are domestic, thus the city's fortunes are heavily tied to the economy. During the late 1990s the stock market reached record highs and unemployment was at a 40-year low, so it wasn't surprising that Vegas did well, too. However, Nevada's economy was already in trouble when terrorists struck the World Trade Center on 9/11. An estimated 15,000 casino workers lost their jobs, and tens of thousands more had their schedules reduced. However, by most accounts, the casino-driven economy has rebounded quicker than other sectors. The proliferation of Internet and Native American–owned casinos is the major challenge to the city's economic supremacy.

SOCIETY & CULTURE

Half of Las Vegans ticked 'white' in the most recent US census. Nearly a quarter claimed Hispanic heritage, with 10% ticking African-American. Asians, Native Americans and Pacific Islanders (including a significant number of transplanted Hawaiians) comprised the bulk of the rest of a rapidly growing minority population.

The vast majority of Las Vegans were born outside Nevada. It's often noted that over 5000 people move here every month; what's less often reported is that another few thousand throw in the towel each month. With so many newcomers, a transient feeling permeates the city. People are very eager (if not desperate) to make new friends.

Sure it's service-oriented by mandate, but everywhere you go people will stop and say hello, and ask if they can help. You should leave town feeling that Sin City has more than its fair share of genuinely friendly residents.

Dos & Don'ts
DRINKING & GAMBLING

Open containers are illegal in public but typically overlooked, except in vehicles. If you're lucky enough to look under 35, carry ID. You can buy booze everywhere 24/7. The legal gambling age is 21.

DRINK DRIVING

Cops crack down on DUIs with a vengeance; fines and sentences are as stiff as the casinos' free drinks are watered down. More people are injured in crosswalks than in auto accidents. Play the smart odds and take a cab.

SMOKING

Cancer sticks are permissible anywhere; stogie puffing is restricted. Restaurants' nonsmoking sections are rarely divided off. There are nonsmoking guestrooms, but no guarantees. One comedian says he loves Vegas because he can savor a cigar in a hospital elevator – full of pregnant women!

ARTS

Like clean government in Chicago, sizzling nightlife in Salt Lake City or real breasts in LA, until recently, cultural arts in Las Vegas would have been just another urban oxymoron. However that's no longer the case.

Architecture

Pre-1950s structures cling to life like a trailer park in a tornado. Vintage hotels are routinely 'imploded' with the machine-gun frequency of Rodney Dangerfield one-liners. The Art Deco Huntridge Performing Arts Theater is the closest thing to an architectural masterpiece.

The consensus is that Las Vegas looks better at night. The Strip's high production value 'architainment' monoliths celebrate nearly everything – except modern-day Nevada. It's quite entertaining to watch impresarios suffering from an edifice complex trying to one-up each other.

Trompe l'oeil and disorientation by design are rampant. Realities are well scripted and foreshortened, featuring set designs cribbed from Hollywood's playbook. All this structural tomfoolery adds up to what may be the world's first metropolitan suburb, where the climate is rendered irrelevant by ubiquitous air-con. Las Vegas is, as Baudelaire described the sensation, the perfect place to 'find solitude in crowds of people.'

Robert Venturi's classic *Learning from Las Vegas* was the first treatise to celebrate Vegas' architecture as pop art. *Viva Las Vegas: After Hours Architecture* by Alan Hess is a well-illustrated history of pre-Luxor properties.

Film & TV

Often said to be the only city in the world with a more distorted sense of reality than Los Angeles, Vegas has long been a favorite shooting location. Casino interiors were cast often by the industry in the 1940s, when Frank Sinatra made his silver-screen debut and movie mogul Howard Hughes frequently worked on location. Atomic testing captured the imagination of B-grade sci-fi directors in the 1950s. Sinatra's Rat Pack enjoyed frequent cameos in the 1960s and Elvis shook his thang in *Viva Las Vegas* (1964). James Bond glorified glitzy Vegas in *Diamonds are Forever* (1971), while Mario Puzo's epic *Godfather* (1972) was the first flick to portray the Mafia in a negative light. As a direct result, directors had difficulty gaining access to casinos until Hal Ashby's *Lookin' to Get Out* (1982) and Albert Brooks' *Lost in America* (1985). In *Rain Man* (1988), Dustin Hoffman and Tom Cruise conspired to beat the house edge. Martin Scorsese broke the silence about 'the organization' with *Casino* (1995).

Robert Redford 'booty calls' Demi Moore – to the dismay of her on-screen hubby Woody Harrelson – in the drama *Indecent Proposal* (1993). Mike Figgis delivered brutal character portrayals in *Leaving Las Vegas* (1995). Joe Eszterhas' *Showgirls* (1995) got two thumbs-down. Obviously infatuated with Sin City, Nicholas Cage starred in *Honeymoon in Vegas* (1992) and the forgettable *Con Air* (1997). The cinematic success of Hunter S Thompson's classic *Fear and Loathing in Las Vegas* (1998) confirmed that sin was in once again. In a remake of the Sinatra classic *Ocean's Eleven* (2001), a star-studded cast plots to bilk a string of casinos.

The hit network show *CSI: Crime Scene Investigation* is a series about police forensic investigations that feature Vegas's neon glow. NBC's drama *Las Vegas* tracks the movements of a surveillance team at a fictional megaresort. Tinseltown is trying to set up a full production shop in Henderson, but the development ran into local opposition from residents who'd rather see Vegas on screen than have the producers in their backyard 24 hours a day.

Great Casino in the Sky

'Should I go to heaven, give me no haloed angels riding snow-white clouds...Give me rather a vaulting red-walled casino with bright lights, bring on horned devils as dealers. Let there be a Pit Boss in the Sky who will give me unlimited credit. And if there is a merciful God in our Universe he will decree that the Player have for all eternity, an Edge against the House.'

Mario Puzo, *Inside Las Vegas*

Literature

Books about Vegas tend to focus on two topics: beating the casinos at their game and doing the town on a dime. Against all odds, editor Mike Tronnes' anthology *Literary Las Vegas* proves that Sin City's follies make for fine literary fodder. Few known authors have hit the jackpot in Vegas, but gonzo journalists such as Tom Wolfe *(The Kandy-Kolored Tangerine-Flake Streamline Baby)*, essayists Joan Didion and Hunter S Thompson *(Fear and Loathing in Las Vegas)*, novelist and screenwriter Mario Puzo *(Inside Las Vegas)* and rock critic Richard Meltzer have all confronted the underbelly of the shimmering beast.

Directory

Dazzling Fremont St at night

ARRIVAL & DEPARTURE

Las Vegas is readily accessible from every major North American city, and, by extension, from most of the world's metropolises. Thirty-five airlines offer non-stop service. Direct flights depart from London, Mexico City, Singapore, Toronto and Tokyo. Check the Web or Sunday travel sections in major newspapers for discounted flights and package deals.

Air
MCCARRAN INTERNATIONAL AIRPORT

Las Vegas is served by McCarran International (LAS; 2, D6; www.mccarran.com) and three general aviation facilities.

Just a crap shoot from the southern end of The Strip, McCarran is one of the world's 10 busiest airports, yet it's easy to navigate. Baggage handling is notoriously slow, but upgrades are in the works. Self-service kiosks ease check-in headaches. Domestic flights use Terminal 1; international and charter flights depart from Terminal 2. A free tram links outlying gates. Pastimes include slot machines, an aviation museum and a 24-hour fitness center. Left luggage lockers are unavailable due to post-9/11 security concerns.

Information

Flight Information	☎ 261-4636
General Inquiries	☎ 261-5211
Parking Information	☎ 261-5121

Airport Access

Taxi fares to Strip hotels (30 minutes max in heavy traffic) run from $10 to $20, cash only. Fares to Downtown average $15 to $25. 'Long-hauling' through the 'airport connector' tunnel is common; tell your driver to use the Paradise Rd surface route unless time is of the essence. Fares include a $1.20 airport tax.

Bell Trans (☎ 800-274-7433, 739-7990; www.bell-trans.com) offers shuttles for $4.75 per person to The Strip, $6 to Downtown. A limousine costs $32 per hour for a chartered sedan or $39 per hour for a luxury six-person stretch limo – a good deal for groups.

If you're traveling light, CAT's bus 109 ($1.25) runs 24/7 to the Transportation Center, a short walk from Downtown hotels.

Bus & Train

The long-distance **Greyhound** (☎ 800-231-2222; www.greyhound.com) buses arrive at the Downtown bus station(3, C3; ☎ 384-9561; 200 S Main St). Talk of reviving the **Amtrak** (☎ 800-872-7245; www.amtrak.com) train service persists, but for now the closest stations are in Needles, CA (106 miles away), Kingman, AZ (123 miles) and Barstow, CA (159 miles). Greyhound provides a daily connecting Thruway motorcoach service between Las Vegas and all three cities. A high-speed MagLev (magnetic levitation) rail link between Southern California and the Vegas Valley is also being studied.

Car & Motorcycle

If not flying, most visitors arrive in their own transport. There's ample free parking and the city's logical street grid is easy to navigate. It's a three-hour drive (145 miles) to Death Valley National Park, three hours (155 miles) to Zion National Park, five hours (267 miles) to Grand Canyon Village, five to six hours (275 miles) to Los Angeles, and seven to eight hours (425 miles) to San Diego. Dial ☎ 877-687-6237 for recorded Nevada road condition updates and ☎ 800-427-7623 for California conditions.

Travel Documents
PASSPORT
Due to heightened security, all foreign visitors must have a passport that has biometric identifiers and is valid for at least six months beyond their planned exit date. Canadians only need proof of citizenship with photo ID.

VISA
Visas are not required for citizens of the reciprocal 27 Visa Waiver Program countries (including Australia, Ireland, New Zealand, the UK and most other European nations), who may enter the US for up to 90 days visa-free. Everyone not covered by the visa-waiver exemption, and those wishing to stay longer, must wrangle a visa from a US embassy or consulate. Double-check the ever-changing requirements at http://travel.state.gov.

RETURN/ONWARD TICKET
Travelers under the reciprocal visa-waiver program need round-trip or onward tickets to enter the US. Travelers applying for visas overseas will generally require such tickets as proof of their intent to skedaddle home.

Customs & Duty Free
Travelers with more than $10,000 in US and/or foreign currency, travelers checks or money orders must declare the money upon entry.

You can import, duty free, 1L of liquor (if you're over 21 years old); 100 cigars (not Cubans), 200 cigarettes or 2kg of tobacco; and gifts totaling $100 ($800 for US citizens).

GETTING AROUND

Since the primary tourist areas are flat, the best way to get around Vegas is on foot, in conjunction with the occasional taxi, trolley, bus or monorail. While you're gumshoeing around town, make sure you stay well hydrated.

Due to exponential growth and stifling traffic congestion, public transit and regional planning are becoming civic priorities. Muggy bus routes serve the sprawling suburbs, but gridlock along The Strip makes navigating the city's core a chore. Air-con private monorails and trolleys also ply The Strip.

Unless otherwise noted, all attractions offer free valet (tip $2) and self-service parking.

Travel Passes
Monorail passes cost for a one/three-day ticket $15/40, or $25 for a 10-ride pass – a good idea if you're staying on The Strip, since one-way rides cost $3. CAT's 24-hour bus passes ($5) are also good-value.

Monorails, Trams, Shuttles
The new private **monorail system** (☎ 699-8200; www.lvmonorail.com; ☯ 6-2am) links properties along The Strip's resort corridor, shuttling between the MGM Grand and the Hilton, Convention Center and the Sahara. At the time of research, the monorail had been out of service for two months due to safety concerns.

A separate free tram system connects Treasure Island and the Mirage; and Excalibur, Luxor and Mandalay Bay. At the time of writing, the free tram between the Bellagio and Monte Carlo was under re-construction.

Most off-Strip hotel-casinos offer free shuttle service to/from The Strip.

Taxi

Although expensive on a per-mile basis, taxis are reasonable on a per-trip basis. A 4½-mile lift from one end of The Strip to the other runs $10 to $15, plus a tip. Taxi stands are at every hotel-casino entrance. Fares (cash only) are metered: flag-fall is $3 plus $1.80 per mile, or 40¢ per minute for waiting. By law, all companies must have at least one wheelchair-accessible van. Reputable companies include **Desert Cab** (☎ 386-9102), **Western** (☎ 736-8000) and **Yellow/Checker/Star** (☎ 873-2000). File complaints via http://taxi.state.nv.us.

Bus

Citizens Area Transit (CAT; ☎ 228-7433; www.catride.com) operates daily 5:30am to 1:30am, with the most-popular Strip and Downtown routes running 24/7; the fare is $2 (exact change required). Free maps and timetables are available from drivers and the Downtown depot (3, D3).

Trolley

Private four-wheeled air-con **trolleys** (☎ 382-1404) ply the length of The Strip, stopping at most hotels. The only detour is to the Hilton on Paradise Rd. Trolleys operate every 15 to 20 minutes daily, 9:30am to 1:30am; the fare is $1.75 and exact change is required. Frequent stops make them the slowest way to get around.

Car & Motorcycle

How you move around Sin City says a lot about who you are. Low-rollers stick to the free or cheap public-transportation options, while high-rollers let it all hang out while cruising in an exotic convertible or stretch Hummer limo. However you roll, free valet and self-parking is abundant, gas is relatively cheap and the traffic moves along at a good clip, except during rush hour on The Strip. Parking is tighter Downtown, but all major properties have lots or garages that are free with validation. Gas costs upwards of $2 per gallon.

ROAD RULES

Drive on the right-hand side of the road. Right-hand turns on red are OK, but avoid blocking intersections at all costs. Buckle up: seat belts are mandatory for all passengers.

The legal blood alcohol level is 0.10%. Most motorists drive conservatively due to the constant presence of traffic cops and harsh fines. Pedestrians supposedly have the right of way. Parking in a blue (handicapped) space carries a $271 minimum fine. Drink-driving violations are rewarded with mandatory jail time, revocation of driving privileges, court fines, raised insurance premiums and lawyers' fees. Beware jaywalkers – more people are injured while crossing the street than in auto accidents.

RENTAL

Economy rates start at around $30 per day and $160 per week, plus $10 to $15 per day for insurance, which is usually optional. Ferraris and exotic convertibles fetch $250 to $750 per day. Most companies require a major credit card, and some require that the driver be at least 25 to 30 years old. Ten percent in local fees are tacked onto rates, plus a 10% airport surcharge. For weekend use, reserve at least two weeks in advance. Airport pick-up and return are complimentary. In most instances, rental cars can be delivered to your hotel.

Agencies with airport desks include **Avis** (☎ 800-831-2847; www .avis.com), **Budget** (☎ 800-527-0700; www.budgetlasvegas.com) and **Thrifty** (☎ 800-367-2277; www .thrifty.com). Most hotels also have rental desks. For something glamorous, ring **Rent-A-Vette** (2, E5; ☎ 800-372-1981; www.rent-a -vette.com; 5021 Swenson St).

Las Vegas Motorcycle Rentals (2, F1; ☎ 877-571-7174; www .lvhd.com; 2605 S Eastern Ave) rents a range of brand new Harleys, from Sportsters ($75 per day) to V-Rods ($200 per day), including unlimited mileage, a helmet and rain suit.

DRIVER'S LICENSE

The only document that you need to operate a car or motorcycle is a license from your home country.

PRACTICALITIES

Climate & When to Go

Consider two crucial criteria when making your travel plans: weather and conventions. The mercury hovers around 100°F June through September. Unless you're on a junket yourself, you'll want to avoid visiting during the biggest conventions. The colossal crowds are annoying – reaching the crab legs at the Big Buffet is never more nerve racking – and it's costly, since hotels jack up room rates.

The slowest time of year is between Thanksgiving and Christmas. If you're claustrophobic, pass on New Year's Eve and major holidays (p87). Most revues shut down the week before Christmas. Hotel rack rates average 10% to 50% less Sunday through Thursday.

Comps & Discounts

The biggest discounts are 'comps' handed out by casinos to members of slot clubs and 'rated' gamblers. 'Full RFB' (room, food and board) is the coveted treatment lavished on the highest rollers (aka 'whales'). See the Gambling section (p26) for the low-down on getting comped and rated – the more you lose, the more you save…

Seniors (over 50 in many cases) and students with ID receive discounts at restaurants and many attractions. While not always extended, children's discounts are more common than family tickets. Freebie magazines distributed in most hotel rooms are the source of the biggest discounts (often half-price or two-for-one admission) on shows, dinner and attractions.

Disabled Travelers

Vegas has the most ADA-accessible guestrooms in the US. Most public transport is also lift-equipped. Wheelchair seating is widely available and assisted listening devices are available at most showrooms.

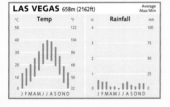

LAS VEGAS 658m (2162ft) Temp / Rainfall — Average Max/Min

Several resort pools have special lifts to enable water access. Contact the Convention & Visitors Authority's ADA coordinator on ☎ 892-7525 (voice relay ☎ 800-326-6888, TTY ☎ 800-326-6868) to request the free *Access Las Vegas* pamphlet. Unless otherwise noted, all attractions in this book are wheelchair-accessible.

Electricity
Adaptors for European plugs are available. Travelers from Asia and Australia should bring adaptors.

Voltage	110-115V
Frequency	60Hz
Cycle	AC
Plugs	two or three pins (two flat pins, often with a round 'grounding' pin)

Embassies & Consulates
Las Vegas has a lot of things, but no consulates or embassies. All embassies are in the nation's capital, Washington, DC; dial ☎ 202-555-1212 for directory assistance. The closest consulates are in Los Angeles and San Francisco.

Emergencies
In general, The Strip is crime free, but beware of pickpockets in crowds and on buses. Police and private security officers are out in force and surveillance cameras are omnipresent. Utilize the in-room safes that are provided by most hotels and make sure you never leave your valuables unattended.

Police, fire, ambulance	☎ 911
Police (nonemergency)	☎ 311 or 229-3111
Alcoholics Anonymous	☎ 598-1888
Gamblers Anonymous	☎ 385-7732
Narcotics Anonymous	☎ 369-3362
Rape Crisis Hotline	☎ 366-1640
Suicide Prevention	☎ 731-2990 or 800-784-2433

Fitness
The age-old question 'participate or spectate?' crops up daily in Sin City. For tips on the best spas and swimming pools, see pp24–5. If you're determined to battle that bulge, try one of the following activities.

GYMS
Most hotels have fitness centers, and the majority of megaresorts have spas (p25). **24-hour Fitness** (1, B4; ☎ 261-3971; 5757 Wayne Newton Blvd, McCarran Airport) and **Las Vegas Athletic Club** (2, E1; ☎ 734-5822; 2655 S Maryland Parkway) are open around the clock; day passes cost $15 to $25.

RUNNING
Since golf courses occupy most of Vegas' green spaces, joggers are stuck with The Strip and arterial roads as their only options – if you're foolhardy enough to brave the heat, poor air quality and maniacal taxis. If you're an inveterate aerobic exerciser, conditions are most favorable in the early morning hours. For something more social, a running club convenes every Wednesday at 6pm at Niketown (p38) in Caesars Forum Shops.

EXTREME SPORTS
Kiwi **AJ Hackett** (2, D2; ☎ 385-4321; www.aj-hackett.com; 810 Circus Circus Dr) was a bungee-jumping pioneer. Take the 52m plunge (from $59) outside the Adventuredome (p21). At **Sky Dive Las Vegas** (☎ 759-3483, 800-875-9348; www.skydivelasvegas.com; 1401 Airport Rd, Boulder City) you can take a tandem 30-second free-fall jump ($155 to $199) after a 20-minute lesson. You'll reach up to 200mph and enjoy a five- to seven-minute parachute glide home.

GOLF
There are dozens of courses in the Vegas Valley, most of which are within 10 miles of The Strip. Call as far ahead as possible to reserve a tee time, or ask your hotel concierge about private courses. The Las Vegas Convention and Visitor's Authority (p91) publishes a free *Las Vegas Golf* guide, or see www .vegasgolfer.com. The municipal **Las Vegas Golf Club** (1, A3; ☎ 646-3003; 4300 W Washington Ave) is open to all comers. Green fees start from $75.

Gay & Lesbian Travelers
Gay Vegas exists, but it's largely unmapped. Despite Mayor Goodman's liberal stance on many social issues, public displays of affection (whether gay or straight) aren't very common or appreciated by the moral majority in this conservative town. The flamboyant Fruit Loop area (2, E5), a mile east of The Strip and near UNLV, is the queer epicenter. See p68 for details.

INFORMATION & ORGANIZATIONS
Pick up a copy of the free *Las Vegas Bugle* (www.lvbugle.com) at **Get Booked** (2, E4; ☎ 737-7780; www .getbooked.com; 4640 S Paradise Rd), the premier gay and lesbian retailer. The **Lambda Business & Professional Association** (2, E1; ☎ 593-2875; www.lambdalv.com; 953 E Sahara Av) is the queer chamber of commerce. **Alternative Lifestyle Commitments** (☎ 888-638-4673) can help arrange same-sex wedding ceremonies.

Health
IMMUNIZATIONS
Visitors from affected areas need to have cholera or yellow-fever immunizations to enter the US.

PRECAUTIONS
Vegas tap water is potable but has a nasty aftertaste, so most locals quaff bottled water. Particulate matter in the air can be quite unpleasant during dust storms. Check the weather before heading outside – searing temperatures take their toll quickly.

MEDICAL SERVICES
The need for insurance when visiting the US cannot be over-emphasized. Excellent medical care is readily available, but it comes at a high price. Doctors often expect payment on the spot for services rendered. Sometimes you'll have to pay up front, and your insurance company will reimburse you.

For medical emergencies dial ☎ 911. The following hospitals have 24-hour emergency facilities. **Sunrise Hospital & Medical Center** (2, F2; ☎ 731-8000, emergency ☎ 731-8080; 3186 Maryland Parkway) **University Medical Center of Southern Nevada** (3, A5; ☎ 383-2000, emergency ☎ 383-2661; 1800 W Charleston Blvd)

DENTAL SERVICES
If you chip a tooth or require emergency dental attention, contact the **Nevada Dental Association** (☎ 800-962-6710; www.nvda .org) for referrals.

PHARMACIES
The following are open 24/7/365: **CVS** (2, C5; ☎ 262-9028; 3758 Las Vegas Blvd S) **Walgreens** (2, C5; ☎ 739-9638; 3765 Las Vegas Blvd S)

Holidays
Holidays marked with an asterisk (*) are widely observed; some are observed the following Monday, if they fall on a weekend.

1 January	New Year's Day*
3rd Monday in January	Martin Luther King Jr Day
3rd Monday in February	Presidents' Day
March/April	Easter Sunday
Last Monday in May	Memorial Day*
4 July	Independence Day*
1st Monday in September	Labor Day*
2nd Monday in October	Columbus Day
11 November	Veterans' Day
4th Thursday in November	Thanksgiving Day*
25 December	Christmas Day*

Imperial System

Americans have managed to avoid the metric system. Distances are measured in feet, yards and miles. Dry weights are measured by the ounce, pound and ton; liquid measures differ from dry measures. Gasoline is dispensed by the US gallon (20% less than the imperial gallon). US pints and quarts are also 20% less than imperial ones.

TEMPERATURE
°C = (°F − 32) ÷ 1.8
°F = (°C x 1.8) + 32

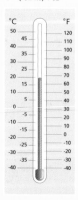

°C	°F
50	120
45	110
40	100
35	90
30	80
25	70
20	60
15	50
10	40
5	30
0	20
-5	10
-10	0
-15	
-20	-10
-25	-20
-30	-30
-35	
-40	-40

DISTANCE
1in = 2.54cm
1cm = 0.39in
1m = 3.3ft = 1.1yd
1ft = 0.3m
1km = 0.62 miles
1 mile = 1.6km

WEIGHT
1kg = 2.2lb
1lb = 0.45kg
1g = 0.04oz
1oz = 28g

VOLUME
1L = 0.26 US gallons
1 US gallon = 3.8L
1L = 0.22 imperial gallons
1 imperial gallon = 4.55L

Internet

Most hotels have business centers that charge an arm and a leg for 24/7 Internet access. Broadband kiosks come and go but wireless is spreading like wildfire. The best WiFi hotspots are off-Strip at the Convention Center and at the airport. Otherwise, your best bet is to kick down for high-speed access in your room. If you've left your laptop at home, the following cafés are your best options.

INTERNET CAFES

Cyber Stop (2, C5; ☎ 736-4782; Hawaiian Marketplace, Polo Towers Plaza, 3743 Las Vegas Blvd S; per hr $12; ⏲ 7-2:30am)

Kinkos (3, C4; ☎ 383-7022; 830 S 4th St; per min 20¢; ⏲ 7am-10pm Mon-Fri) WiFi hotspot.

Kinkos (2, D4; ☎ 951-2400; Tropicana, 395 Hughes Center Dr; per min 20¢; ⏲ 24/7/365) WiFi hotspot.

INTERNET SERVICE PROVIDERS

Major ISP dial-up access numbers include **AOL** (☎ 505-4266, 932-2500), **AT&T** (☎ 374-0010, 266-0003) and **Earthlink** (☎ 289-4078, 358-0020).

USEFUL WEBSITES

The Lonely Planet website (www.lonelyplanet.com) has Sin City links and details. Other good sites to surf include:

Vegas.com (www.vegas.com)

Las Vegas.com (www.lasvegas.com)

Las Vegas' official site (www.ci.las -vegas.nv.us)

Las Vegas Advisor (www.lasvegas advisor.com)

Las Vegas Weekly (www.lasvegas weekly.com)

LVCVA (www.vegasfreedom.com)

Lost Property

Ask for security at hotels for lost-and-found services. Ring **CAT** (☎ 228-7488) customer service for items lost on buses.

Money
CURRENCY

US currency (the dollar) is the only one accepted in Vegas. It's divided into 100 cents (¢). Coins come in 1¢ (penny), 5¢ (nickel), 10¢ (dime), 25¢ (quarter), 50¢ (half-dollar; these are rare) and $1 denominations. Notes come in $1, $2 (also rare), $5, $10, $20, $50 and $100.

TRAVELERS CHECKS

Checks issued by **American Express** (☎ 800-528-4800) and **Thomas Cook** (☎ 800-287-7362) are accepted by most businesses and can be easily replaced if they are lost or stolen. Restaurants, hotels and most shops readily accept US dollar checks. Fast-food restaurants and smaller off-Strip businesses will sometimes refuse to accept checks.

CREDIT CARDS

MasterCard, Visa (both of which are affiliated with European Access Cards) and American Express are widely accepted. Less accepted are Discover and Diners Club. All casinos will advance cash against plastic, but fees are sky-high. For lost cards, contact:

American Express	☎ 800-992-3404
Diners Club	☎ 800-234-6377
Discover	☎ 800-347-2683
MasterCard	☎ 800-307-7309
Visa	☎ 800-336-8472

ATMS

Every hotel-casino, bank and most convenience stores have ATMs. Plus, Cirrus and Instant-Teller are the biggest networks. You'll be charged to use ATMs other than your own bank's (starting at $1). Most machines will disclose the amount and ask whether you want to proceed before dispensing the dough.

CHANGING MONEY

Casinos exist to separate you from your dough and thus will facilitate that end any way they can. Fees at casinos to exchange foreign currency tend to be higher than at banks but lower than at exchange bureaus. **American Express** (2, C3; ☎ 739-8474; Fashion Show Mall, 3200 Las Vegas Blvd S) changes currencies at competitive rates.

Newspapers & Magazines

Nevada's largest daily newspaper is the conservative *Las Vegas Review-Journal* (www.lvrj.com), which hits the streets every morning and publishes the Friday *Neon* entertainment guide. The *Las Vegas Sun* (www.lasvegassun.com) is the afternoon rag. Free tabloid weeklies include *CityLife* (www.lasvegascitylife.com), *Las Vegas Weekly* (www.lasvegasweekly.com) and *Las Vegas Mercury* (www.lasvegasmerecury.com). Major US dailies are available at hotels. The glossy monthly *Casino Player* (www.casinoplayer.com) magazine targets gaming enthusiasts.

Opening Hours

Open 24/7/365 is the rule – many places don't even bother with locks on their doors. Government office hours are weekdays 9am to 5pm; shop hours are 10am to 10pm (later on weekends). Christmas is one of the few holidays for which most shops close.

Photography & Video

Print film is widely available at hotel gift shops, supermarkets and drugstores; 35mm slide film is harder to find. Camera shops stock B&W film. If you purchase a video, note that the US uses the NTSC color TV standard, which is not compatible with international standards like PAL and Secam. Photographing in casinos is strongly discouraged and is prohibited at McCarran Airport.

Post

There are full-service post offices at Caesars Forum Shops (2, C4; Caesars Palace, 3500 Las Vegas Blvd S; ☺ 10am-11pm); McCarran Airport (2, E6; ☺ 9am-5pm); and just west of The Strip (2, C2; ☎ 735-8519; 3100 S Industrial Rd; ☺ 8:30am-5pm Mon-Sat).

POSTAL RATES

Stamps are available at hotel front desks, lobby sundries shops and some ATMs. Domestic rates are 37¢ for letters up to 1oz (plus 23¢ for each additional ounce) and 23¢ for postcards. International airmail rates are 70¢ for letters of the same size and postcards. Postcards to Canada and Mexico cost 50¢.

Radio

No fewer than five AM sports-talk stations feed the insatiable appetite of this sports-betting paradise. News-talk stations (which also cover sports) with frequent traffic and weather reports include KDWN (720AM) and KXNT (840AM). FM is dominated by country and western, with KWNR (95.5FM) at the head of the herd. National Public Radio affiliate KNPR (89.5FM) spins classical between news breaks. The University of Nevada's (UNLV) noncommer-cial radio station KUNV (91.5FM) is Southern Nevada's jazz spot.

Telephone

Public phones are mostly coin-operated; some accept credit cards. Payphones are widespread, despite the expansion of cellular coverage. Local calls generally cost 35¢. If dialing a number outside your area, dial ☎ 1 first. Major carriers like **AT&T** (☎ 800-321-0288) facilitate long-distance calls.

PHONECARDS

Pharmacies and convenience stores sell prepaid phonecards, but they can be rip-offs – check the fine print for hidden fees and surcharges.

MOBILE PHONES

The US uses a variety of mobile-phone systems including GSM, which is remotely compatible with systems used outside of North America. Most North American visitors can use their phones in Vegas, but check with your carrier about roaming charges before you start racking up the minutes. On The Strip, Cyber Stop (p88) rents Nokia handsets ($5 per day plus 85¢ per minute for calls).

COUNTRY & CITY CODES

USA	☎ 1
Southern Nevada	☎ 702
Rest of Nevada	☎ 775

INTERNATIONAL CODES

Dial ☎ 011 followed by:

Australia	☎ 61
Canada	☎ 1
France	☎ 33
Germany	☎ 49
Japan	☎ 81
New Zealand	☎ 64
South Africa	☎ 27
UK	☎ 44

USEFUL PHONE NUMBERS

Operator	☎ 0
International Operator	☎ 00
Collect (reverse-charge)	☎ 0
Operator-Assisted Calls	☎ 01
Local Directory Inquiries	☎ 411
Time & Weather	☎ 248-4800

TV

Major broadcast networks (ABC, CBS, FOX and NBC) offer familiar prime-time fare; alternatives include public affairs on the university's public-access channel (UNLV-TV) and Public Broadcasting Service (PBS). Cable in most hotels is limited to CNN news, ESPN sports and pay-per-view movies; better hotels offer satellite stations via DirecTV.

Time

Las Vegas uses Pacific Standard Time (PST), which is 8hrs behind Greenwich Mean Time (GMT). Daylight-saving starts on the first Sunday in April, when the clocks move forward one hour; it finishes the last Sunday in October. At noon in Vegas it's:

3pm in New York
7pm in Cape Town
8pm in London
9pm in Paris
3am (following day) in Sydney

Tipping

Hotel and casino staffers rely on tips to bring their incomes up to decent levels. Fortunes have been made by valet parking concession owners. However, only give tips as a reward for good service. Use the following list to figure out how much to give:

Airport skycaps at least $1 per bag
Bellhops $1 to $2 per bag
Change persons 10% of winnings when a slot machine pays off
Cocktail servers 10% to 15%; if drinking for free in a casino, $1 per round
Concierges nothing for info, up to $20 for securing tickets to a sold-out show
Hotel maids up to $5 per day
Restaurants 15% to 20% (not expected in fast-food, takeout or self-serve places)
Taxis and limos 10% to 15%
Valet parking $2 when handed the keys

Tourist Information

Many tour operators push unofficial 'visitor information,' but there's only one official tourist office. The **Las Vegas Convention & Visitors Authority hotline** (LVCVA; ☎ 892-7575) has helpful operators and recorded entertainment and convention schedules.
Las Vegas Convention & Visitors Authority Visitor Information Center (2, D2; ☎ 892-0711, 877-847-4858; www.vegasfreedom.com; 3150 Paradise Rd; ☽ 8am-5pm)

Women Travelers

Women need not be too concerned about traveling solo here. On The Strip, drunk men may make harassing comments, but most won't take their obnoxious behavior further if you ignore them. Like it or not, 'working girls' (aka 'escorts') are a part of Nevada's high-rolling culture. However, since prostitution is illegal in Clark County, women are unlikely to be subjected to unwanted propositions.

Tampons and pads are widely available, although the selection is smaller than in Europe or Australia. The contraceptive pill is widely available but only by prescription. Emergency contraception services are available without a prescription from **Planned Parenthood** (1, B3; ☎ 878-7776; 3220 W Charleston Blvd), which is also located on Flamingo Rd (1, B4; ☎ 547-9888; 3320 E Flamingo Rd).

Index

See also separate indexes for Eating (p94), Sleeping (p94), Shopping (p94) and Sights with map references (p95).

Sight Index

FEATURES

[El Sombrero Café] .... *Eating*
[Olympic Garden] .... *Entertainment*
[Hush] .... *Drinking*
[Treasure Island] .... *Highlights*
[The Attic] .... *Shopping*
[Neon Museum] .... *Sights/Activities*
[THEhotel] .... *Sleeping*

AREAS

.... Building
.... Land
.... Mall
.... Other Area
.... Park/Cemetary
.... Sports
.... Urban

HYDROGRAPHY

.... River, Creek
.... Intermittent River
.... Water

BOUNDARIES

.... State, Provincial
.... Regional, Suburb

ROUTES

.... Tollway
.... Freeway
.... Primary Road
.... Secondary Road
.... Tertiary Road
.... Lane
.... Under Construction
.... One-Way Street
.... Unsealed Road
.... Mall/Steps
.... Tunnel
.... Walking Path
.... Walking Trail
.... Track
.... Walking Tour

TRANSPORT

.... Airport, Airfield
.... Rail
.... Tram

SYMBOLS

.... Bank, ATM
.... Christian
.... Embassy, Consulate
.... Hospital, Clinic
.... Information
.... Internet Access
.... Lookout
.... Monument
.... Mountain, Volcano
.... National Park
.... Parking Area
.... Petrol Station
.... Picnic Area
.... Point of Interest
.... Police Station
.... Post Office
.... Telephone
.... Toilets
.... Zoo, Bird Sanctuary
.... Waterfall

24/7 travel advice
www.lonelyplanet.com